Advance P₁
Eat the El

Entertaining, poignant and informative only begin to describe author Karolyn Blume's message in *Eat the Elephant: Overcoming Overwhelm*. From the first page to the last, Karolyn keeps readers engaged with practical information. Throughout the book she shares stories to make important points; stories that are memorable and touching. Pulling from her own experiences, Karolyn shows exactly how to overcome overwhelm while actually enjoying the process.

This book is a must read for anyone who is in overwhelm and desperately seeks a usable solution. Two thumbs up!

Kathleen Gage
Business consultant
Power Up for Profits

Eat the Elephant is an overwhelmingly obvious book everyone needs to read because we all face overwhelm in our lives and many of us do every day. Karolyn Blume gives you real-life, practical, easy-to-use strategies to increase your productivity in a stress-free way that you can use today, tomorrow and for the rest of your life. *Eat the Elephant* is a well-written, fun read, done in a no-nonsense manner you'll love... And, be sure to read the preface!

Diane Conklin
President/Founder
www.CompleteMarketingSystems.com

As a long time career coach, I've seen how the hunger for achievement and success can easily devolve into lack of clarity and overwhelm. *Eat the Elephant* is a long overdue wake-up call about the insidious effects of overwhelm and a relief-giving method for overcoming it. Written from a basis of experience and empathy, this book will make a difference in your life.

Dawn Lennon
Author of *Business Fitness:
The Power to Succeed—Your Way*

Overwhelm grabs us all by the throat and drags us down in these fast-paced days. *Eat the Elephant* is an excellent, actionable guide to subduing that relentless attacker and reducing the insidious pressures of modern life.

Lynn Jordan
Publishing and promotion consultant
IndiePublishingSuccess.com

A lawyer who is as witty as she is wise... yeah, really. *Eat the Elephant* instantly transforms your relationship with overwhelm in your life or business with humor and compassion. "Overwhelm as messy thoughts, not messy circumstances" immediately tells you that this is much more than "clearing your clutter," it's opening your life to have more of what you want, easily... and now.

Chris Makell
"Courage In Business" speaker and author of
A Smack Upside the Head and *Courage Is the New GREEN*
www.ChrisMakell.com

Eat the Elephant was exactly what I was looking for! Nothing is more overwhelming than receiving a traumatic diagnosis. Understanding that there are tools and strategies to help unravel the overwhelm, not only in regards to a serious illness, but overwhelm that occurs in everyday life, is the first and most important step in preserving our own personal health. I recommend all my clients incorporate the tools presented in *Eat the Elephant* to ensure the best results on their journey to regain and maintain great health.

Marika Hamilton
Founder of Dealing with Healing
www.dealingwithhealing.com

Eat the Elephant – only Karolyn could take this topic and bring it to life. With her humor and no-nonsense approach to life's situations, she is able to hit the target squarely and make you wonder why you weren't able to see it before.

Sally M. Handlon
President
Handlon Business Resources LLC

Eat the Elephant provides the needed tool set to help achieve personal and professional success. Setting measurable goals is a learned skill set and an invaluable tool, however the information presented in *Eat the Elephant* is the secret weapon to attaining maximum results while mitigating the stress and overwhelm that accompany today's busy life. This is a must read for any business owner looking to develop leaders from within.

Brian Meeks
President
Out to Lunch, Inc.

For some years now I have postponed a major personal undertaking because, truthfully, it is so overwhelming that I get anxious and depressed just thinking about it let alone having the willpower and desire to tackle it. With the tips and lifestyle changes offered in *Eat the Elephant*, I am now on my path. I feel I have a "roadmap" to help me on my way to better manage my life, take on challenges and still keep me on an even keel.

Joan M. Juliano
Senior Registered Client Associate

Eat the Elephant is an enjoyable read that offers a wealth of great suggestions and exercises. Written with humor and clarity, this book walks you through how to rid yourself of procrastination, perfectionism, and many other plagues of the modern world. You can read this book quickly, and you'll get helpful nuggets; if you choose to go through it slowly, it has the potential for lasting transformation. Altogether a marvelous contribution to the literature designed to make our lives better!

Pamela Bruner
Business coach
Author of *Tapping into Ultimate Success*

In *Eat the Elephant: Overcoming Overwhelm* Karolyn Vreeland Blume, like a good friend, offers personal stories, tough love and practical advice – all with a sense of humor that is contagious. *Eat the Elephant* will show you the benefit of taking a compassionate approach to your overwhelm tendencies so you are better able to transform them.

Louise Phipps Senft
Author of *Being Relational: The Seven Ways* and co-founder
of ORANS: a social movement for relational living

Anyone who is living in 2015 can and will identify with *Eat the Elephant* and its core messages. The trick is we all need to adapt the solutions! Refreshing in her no-nonsense approach and humorous writing style, Karolyn Vreeland Blume delivers sound advice for anyone and everyone without burying the reader in a morass of studies and statistics. This book is not just fun to read – it is a must read for people who want to find a path and make a plan that allows them to take each day, each task, each challenge apart and step out of the world of overwhelm.

Nancy Van Duyne
Vice President
Congressional Affairs

Karolyn Blume is a remarkable woman and shares her insights and knowledge with us in a frank and compassionate voice. She leads each reader on the path out of the chaos that being overwhelmed produces and assists in the move from anxiety to inner peace and self-understanding. If you are like me and get overwhelmed easily, this book is for you.

Nan Waller Burnett, MA
transformative, high conflict mediator, psychotherapist, conflict systems design consultant, conflict coach, author of a daily spiritual practice book entitled *Calm in the Face of the Storm: Spiritual Daily Practice for the Peacemaker,* and winner of a National Independent Book Publishers Award for spirituality and inspiration

Karolyn Blume shines a spotlight on the elephant in the room but she doesn't leave us alone with it. With this book, based on her knowledge, experience and good old common sense, she can help anyone overcome the overwhelm and take back their life. I found her tips and ideas practical and straightforward while her sense of humor made it feel like a trusted friend was in the room with me. I'm recommending *Eat the Elephant* to my clients but they'll have to buy their own. My personal copy is staying close by just in case that elephant tries to edge its way back into my life.

Aprille Janes
Bolder Business Coach
www.BolderBiz.com

In elegant and practical language, Karolyn Blume describes what it's like to succumb to overwhelm – but she also offers a viable and "doable" path to clarity and peace. If you struggle with overwhelm and stress, this book will move you, once and for all, beyond resistance and procrastination toward the life you've always dreamed about. It's possible, and Karolyn is an excellent guide.

Michele Woodward
Author and executive coach
www.michelewoodward.com

Karolyn Vreeland Blume tells it like it is. She's been there, done that, and found her way through the morass. The insights, experience and resources she shares comfort sufferers of overwhelm and pave the way to relief. Karolyn is funny, compassionate, straight forward, and entertaining. You will love her after the first "bite" of *Eat the Elephant*!

Maureen Fahey Knutson
Founder and CEO
Fireworks Transformations

EAT
the Elephant

Overcoming Overwhelm

Karolyn Vreeland Blume

THOMAS NOBLE
BOOKS

Permissions Department
Thomas Noble Books
427 N Tatnall Street #90946
Wilmington, DE 19801-2230

This publication is designed to provide accurate and authoritative information in regard to the subject matter covered. It is sold with the understanding that the author is not engaged in rendering professional services. If legal, accounting, medical, psychological, or any other expert assistance is required, the services of a competent professional person should be sought.

Library of Congress Control Number: 2015931238

ISBN: 978-0-9892357-8-5
Printed in the United States of America

Editing by Gwen Hoffnagle

Cover design and internal design by David Redondo

For my daughter, Susanna, the joy of my life, whose brilliant mind and compassionate heart are a constant source of inspiration and pride.

ACKNOWLEDGMENTS

As is always the case, I stand on the shoulders of others in this venture. Mere words cannot express my gratitude to each person who gave assistance and support on this journey, and I humbly express my thanks here.

To my publisher, Lynne Klippel of Thomas Noble Books, whose patience with a headstrong rookie author made this a wonderful experience. To my editor, Gwen Hoffnagle, who respected my quirkiness and unique style. To David Redondo, who developed a cover that I love.

To Kathleen Gage, my mentor, for teaching me everything I know about book launches, and the Power Partners mastermind group – Alli, Aprille, Kimberly, Lana, Lynn J., Lynn T., Marika, and Maureen – for their support and encouragement from the first glimmer of the idea to the end result.

To Terry Loving for masterfully handling the complexities of launching this book and keeping me on task for a terrific launch.

To my good friend and mentor, Diane Conklin, who tolerated my overwhelm, indecision, and general stubbornness to help me build a business I am proud of.

To all my beta readers whose support and endorsements confirmed my commitment to put my words to paper.

To my mother, Peggy Vreeland, for keeping tabs on my progress. Mom, I always told you it was harder to write books than to read them. Thanks for hanging in. To my sister, Ticia Vreeland, my niece Whitney McGowan, and my nephew Doug Vreeland for their support.

To Peter Blume for sharing his experiences with book publishing and saving me time and stress along the way.

To Garret and Betsy Vreeland for lending me their house at the Jersey shore to finish writing, and for their encouragement and interest in the progress of this book.

To my nephew and nieces, Luke, Annie, and Meg Vreeland, for their constant encouragement and suggestions.

And to my daughter, Susanna Blume, who was instrumental in the idea for this book and held the balloon strings throughout the highs and lows along the way. You make it all worthwhile every day, for which you will always be the joy of my life.

Thank you all.

TABLE OF CONTENTS

PREFACE

My daughter tells me that nobody reads the prefaces of books, but I'll take my chances, and make it short and sweet. Before you begin reading *Eat the Elephant*, you might want to pick up a few tools to make the process more productive. Think of it as a shopping list for your personal development.

First, if you don't already have a nice journal, get one. Hold it in your hands, feel the weight and texture of the paper, the strength of the binding, the comfort of the pen on the page. Get a journal that you will want to use, and then use it.

If you are reading the hard copy of the book, get yourself a highlighter and some Post-it® flags to mark passages you want to refer to later. I use a combination device by Post-it that has a highlighter on one end, a pen on the other end, and flags on the side. It is one tool that does all I need, and I use it all the time.

You will need a box of crayons or colored pencils for several of the exercises. Get at least twenty-four different colors. Get some comfortable pens for journal writing. While you're at the office supply store, get a few nice pads of paper or spiral-bound notebooks. I use a spiral-bound notebook that's about 9" x 7" called a project planner, which has a small column on the left-hand side of each page for action items, and the rest of the page is for writing lists, notes, etc.

For those of you reading on an e-reader who want hard copies of the exercises, go to www.KarolynBlume.com for free downloads. There is also a resource page on the website for further information about some of the topics covered in *Eat the Elephant*.

Most important, enjoy your journey through the book. Whether you like it or not, please post a review on social media and at Amazon.com. You can also email me at Karolyn@EatTheElephantBook.com, and I'll try to respond to all posts.

Q: *Why did the elephants get kicked out of the pool?*

A: *They couldn't keep their trunks up.*

1
GETTING STARTED

"The pain pushes you until the vision pulls you."
—Michael Beckwith

Congratulations! By buying *Eat the Elephant* you have taken your first step toward emerging from the pressure and pain of overwhelm. You have recognized the problem and chosen to do something about it. In the following pages you will take a journey through the past, present, and future to learn strategies for overcoming overwhelm and the pitfalls you might encounter. Like so many personal development authors, I write what I need to learn. This book is a result of my own journey through overwhelm. The pain was so great and the reliable information so scattered that I had to create my own solution by combining education, life experience, research, and training.

As a personal development provocateur, I help my clients navigate the stormy seas of life and business by asking questions. Lots of questions. As I often say, "Sometimes there's a method to my madness and sometimes it is just madness." In *Eat the Elephant*, I assure you, there is definitely a reason for all the questions.

Overwhelm has become a way of life. Most people are so used to it that they don't even think about it until they reach total overload and break down. At that point the problem seems so huge that there is no way to know how to dig out of it. It seems easier to stay in bed and pull the covers over your head. That, however, is not a solution. It is avoidance.

Several years ago I moved from a 2,600 square foot house to a 1,300 square foot house. Although I had gotten rid of half my stuff, there was still so much that when the movers left one of them handed me a box of tissues and told me I would need them. There was not one room that wasn't stuffed with stuff. It was like a nightmare episode of *Hoarders*. I was a wreck, and the overwhelm was devastating.

What did I do? I crawled into bed, pulled the covers over my head, and stayed there for thirty-six hours until my daughter and two friends called a halt to my pity party. From the looks on their faces they understood my pain, but were having none of it. We went to a neighborhood Mexican restaurant for enchiladas and margaritas, and when I returned home I had a more positive outlook on the situation. Mind you, the moving fairies didn't sneak in and unpack any boxes, but my mindset had improved considerably.

I needed a strategy. I sat on the floor (the furniture was covered with boxes) and observed my surroundings. Rather than seeing 1,300 square feet of unpacked boxes, I saw each individual room as a project, and each box an individual task. What was most important to me? It was to have one room, a safe haven if you will, where I could relax and not be surrounded by boxes and chaos. I chose the bedroom, and began unpacking one box at a time. I did nothing else, thought of nothing else – just the one box I was working on at the moment.

When the bedroom was clear of all the boxes, I admired my good work and celebrated my new bedroom. Then I chose the second room – the kitchen – and did the same thing, one box at a time. After a couple of weeks, most of the boxes were gone and my outlook had improved considerably. I kept reminding myself that whatever I put away could be rearranged. Nothing was permanent. The unpacking did not have to be perfect! I could place things where they made sense and move them later if necessary.

When I realized that the key to tackling a big job was to chunk it down into smaller, more manageable ones, the Eat-the-Elephant strategy became real. It took time to develop the tools to maximize its effectiveness, and there was lots of angst in working through the oppressive overwhelm I felt. I was unsatisfied in my work, unhappy with relationships, and absent too often from my family. All the while

I felt like a hamster on a wheel, running faster and faster but getting nowhere. My life was a giant-sized game of Whac-A-Mole.

But I kept trying. I was sure that if I just worked harder, managed my time better, or was a better person, all the frustration of overwhelm would go away. Well, my friends, that's a crock. No matter how hard I worked or how long I worked, the feelings of inadequacy never went away. It wasn't until I hit the bottom of my psychic barrel and began to look at my life differently that I saw the path toward overcoming overwhelm and finding a life I loved. This is what I want for you. Why should you suffer pain and frustration when there's a strategy that can help you navigate your way out of overwhelm?

It is easy in this day and age to be overwhelmed by life. Research shows that you are bombarded with over 3,000 messages every day: do this, buy that, sign up for something else – not to mention news reports, sports scores, advertisements, websites, celebrity gossip, media, etc. No wonder you feel overwhelmed. All of these messages are delivered with the same intensity and the same level of importance and urgency. There is no easy way to know what's important and what's not. But don't worry, you don't have to review all 3,000; that would be impossible. Learn to be your own filter by deciding what's important to you, focusing on those things, and ignoring the rest.

The good news is that you have instant access to incredible amounts of information on the web – information that used to require hours of research, trips to the library, fact-finding skills, and a lot of time. Now, thanks to the Internet and powerful search engines, at the click of a mouse you have access to all kinds of people, places, and things. You can find out who sang the song that you can't seem to get out of your head. You can learn about life in a faraway land. You can buy virtually anything with a click and a credit card.

But these giant strides in technology and access do not come without pitfalls. With over 3,000 marketing messages per day, how do you triage them so you'll know which need your attention and which do not? Advertisers want to capture your attention with louder, more colorful, or bigger messages. And some of them are very clever. But they're distractions that divert your attention from your agenda to the messenger's agenda. With all those distractions it is no wonder that you don't accomplish what you set out to do. You don't want to miss anything, or maybe something looks interesting or important. Some or all of those things might be true. But exploring them is still taking away from what you set out to do.

There are also the more insidious distractions like email and social media. There are people who spend hours a day on social media, which is fine as long as you have no life. Social media is a great tool for building a business, keeping in touch with friends, or exploring new ideas. But it is just that: a tool, not a lifestyle. The same is true with email. At the push of a button your message is sent to someone across the street or around the world in seconds. What a marvelous tool! It sure beats writing your ideas on a piece of paper, putting it in an envelope, finding the correct postage, locating the recipient's address and zip code, driving to the post office, and waiting days for a response. Ah, the good old days! But email is also a way for others to make you a part of their underlying agenda. It forces you to be a reactor, not an actor in your own life. Exactly how many cat videos can any one person watch?

The Internet is not going away, thank goodness. The relentless pace of life will not diminish. The distractions will increase just as they have for years, and the demands on your time will become more burdensome if you don't take action now to get your life and your freedom back. You can see a new approach is needed. The days of business as usual ended when business became unusual. The days of a nine-to-five workday are a thing of the past. Global markets and the ability to do business in multiple time zones through the Internet have radically changed the environment.

You may feel that overwhelm has made your life a living hell. But the door to a living hell swings both ways. You can choose to pass through to the other side. Although you might not have chosen to walk through the entrance, you and only you have the choice to walk through the exit. I have already made that journey and want to help you make yours with as little pain as possible. But there will be pain. Growth comes only through change, and change is painful. But with the exercises I provide you can prepare yourself to do the work and reap the reward.

Overwhelm is a family affair. Although you might think you are disguising your pain and frustration, I assure you that you aren't that good an actor. Although those around you might not know exactly what is bothering you, they know something is, and they might not be as compassionate as you would like. Even the most conflict-averse people can pick a fight when faced with behavior they don't understand.

I used to think my life was unique; that no one, not even my siblings, had the same experiences I had. But the longer I've been around and the more people I've spoken with, the more I've realized that most people think their childhoods were crappy in at least some respect.

Crappy can be defined in many ways – usually by the victims through the stories they tell themselves. Aside from major trauma such as physical or sexual abuse, most of us have suffered emotional abuse of some kind and degree. It might be lack of attention from one or both parents, constant belittling, excessive criticism, lack of support, lack of nurturing, authoritarian parents, sibling rivalry, or any one of hundreds of other actions or inactions experienced while growing up. We continue to carry the scars of those experiences with us into adulthood.

How you deal with those scars from the past as an adult makes all the difference in the quality of your life going forward. Sensitive people tend to have a more difficult time coming to grips with their personal histories than rough-and-tumble folks; but even if you think you're tough, you're not immune to the lasting effects of childhood trauma.

It is a constant source of amazement to me how we weave the stories of our youth into our psyches long after the glow of youth wanes. We tell ourselves the same stories over and over, which gives them much more power than they deserve.

While that last sentence might seem fairly obvious, it took me a long time to figure out. Once I did, however, I knew I had to share the insight I had gleaned with others who could benefit from my work. Often our response to overwhelm has its roots in how we perceive the world and our place in it. In order to eat the elephant, figure out where you sabotage yourself by carrying the mantle of past perceptions. This work is based on my experiences, research, trial and error, experimentation, frustration, and a healthy dose of stubborn persistence.

On occasion you might not like what I tell you in *Eat the Elephant*, but it is not in my nature to pussyfoot around (lawyers don't pussyfoot) or sugarcoat the truth. Candor does not mean being unkind or launching personal attacks to get your point across, but I am direct. I won't waste your time and I will cut years off your learning curve. I call 'em like I see 'em.

An important thing I learned on this journey is to make time to care for yourself. As you make choices about what to spend your time and energy on, put self-care at the top of the list. All too often women take care of the rest of the world before they tend to their own well-being. Just like flight attendants say on every flight, put your own mask on before you help others; you can't serve the world until you serve yourself. For most of my life I thought that sentiment was totally selfish; however, now, in my dotage, I realize how supportive of my well-being it is.

In order to serve others, stand for something larger than yourself and give from a generous heart. If you can't be generous with yourself, you can't be generous to others. I can only give to you now because I have taken care of myself and have something to share with you, though I am still a work in progress and hopefully always will be. Allow me to share what I've learned with you. I believe that when the student is ready, the teacher will appear. If you're ready, I am here for you.

This book is yours. It does not belong to a library or friend (I hope). Use it as the resource it is. Underline, highlight, make marginal notes, dog-ear pages, use flags and Post-its – top, bottom, and side; no one will see but you. Fully engage in the material, think through it, curse me out if necessary; but know that all of the information comes to you from my heart. Feel free to revisit chapters or passages that intrigue or frustrate you.

A word of explanation about the title of this book: There is an old children's joke that I remember from my youth. "How do you eat an elephant?" And the answer is, "One bite at a time." In first grade I thought that was hilarious. Now I know that it is the secret to overcoming the pain of overwhelm. I use this technique any time I have a big project to do, or even when cooking Thanksgiving dinner. Once you get the hang of it, the system can be adapted to suit most situations.

Don't let the summons to eat the elephant scare you; I will be with you all the way. Grab your knife and fork and don't worry; it tastes like chicken.

Let's dig right in.

Q: *What is big and gray and wears a mask?*

A: *The elephantom of the opera.*

2 THE BIG "O"

"Seek peace. When you have peace within,
real peace with others will be possible."

—Thich Nhat Hanh

In the twenty-first century, we have resources and opportunities that we could not have imagined twenty years ago, or even ten years ago. Mass communication is instant; virtually unlimited information is available at the click of a mouse. You can communicate with anyone on the planet, and there is a twenty-four-hour news cycle. The resources we have at our fingertips are mind-boggling. But all of these opportunities bring problems, too.

Overwhelm – the big "O" – is everywhere. Not a day goes by when we don't think of or hear about overwhelm. It is in the news, on television, on social media, in conversations around the water cooler, in boardrooms, bedrooms, coffee shops – everywhere. It is the cause of quiet desperation for millions of people the world over, and continues to increase in epidemic proportions. If overwhelm were a disease, which some argue it is, governments and researchers would dedicate limitless resources in finding a cure. Why aren't they?

The conventional wisdom is to just "suck it up," or "live with it," or "everybody is in the same boat," or "put on your big girl panties and deal," or "why should your life be different from everybody else's?" or "it's the way things are today." There are too many choices – I have 1,000 channels on cable TV, which somehow makes it even harder to choose one to watch.

Are we resigned to endure the stress and misery of feeling constantly overwhelmed? I don't think so! But we need new techniques for dealing with the demands that all of the great resources and opportunities impose on us. The good news is that there are strategies you can learn for reducing the burden of overwhelm in a very short time – sometimes instantly.

You are not broken! There is nothing wrong with you. You don't need to be fixed. You are not feeling anything that you can't change with help and guidance from someone who has been where you are now. As we will discuss later, overwhelm is the result of messy thoughts, not messy circumstances. Become aware of the possibilities that exist, then take action on what is offered. It sounds simple, and it is. This is not rocket science. There are no tricks, no sleight of hand or mind. But it is not easy. Like anything worthwhile, it takes work and commitment. If you follow the plan in *Eat the Elephant*, by the end of the book you will have techniques to tackle any task, even the most daunting ones.

We'll examine the challenges everyone faces in this complex world and learn why they stump us. We'll explore opportunities to take control of your timeline and your life, and provide solutions for the problems that keep you from accomplishing what you want to do.

THE PROGRESSION OF OVERWHELM

While everyone experiences overwhelm differently, often it evolves from overwhelm to burnout, which is a complete absence of hope. The progression goes like this:

1. You have a vision for your life or a project to accomplish that becomes a mission, and you become emotionally attached to the outcome. It might be a result of your desire to help people, do a good job, contribute to society, or serve a higher purpose. Perhaps it is an important project at work, an issue you feel strongly about that is now before the school board, or a calling to work on climate change. It can be a combination of many interests or projects that you care about.

2. You enlist your tribe to help you. You generate ideas for the execution of the project. Maybe your vision is vast and sweeping in the beginning and you haven't fully developed the process.

3. Because you are so attached to the outcome, you feel you need to control all aspects of the project.

4. You work very hard, sometimes without a clear focus on the exact steps that need to be taken in turn. At this point, it would be beneficial if you knew how to work smarter rather than harder.

5. You are pushing against the tide rather than being open and going with the flow. You feel as if you are in a constant riptide pulling you in the opposite direction from your goal.

6. You frequently feel discontent or anger with the project and those involved for no apparent reason.

7. Working constantly to the exclusion of family, friends, and self-care leads to isolation.

8. Your life loses its meaning and purpose. This is the point at which abuse of drugs, alcohol, sex, gambling, or shopping might offer you compensation for the loss.

9. You feel exhausted all the time, even after a good night's sleep. Hauling yourself out of bed becomes a monumental task because your life is filled with dread that you can't bear to face.

Notice I didn't say "won't face"; I said "can't face." The choice is no longer there; you are physically and emotionally unable to face your life.

10. You are depressed and hopeless. Without hope your life is not worth living and you see no escape from intolerable misery.

11. Total collapse overtakes you and you are unable to function. You don't eat, bathe, dress, engage with other people, or feel any emotion other than despair. Even the anger that you used to feel is gone. There is nothing left.

12. You totally burn out knowing that your situation is hopeless, and unable to seek help, you give up. You might feel that suicide is the only way to stop the pain.

If you believe that your situation falls in categories 9 or above, I urge you to see a mental health professional immediately. I am not trained in psychiatry or psychology, and this book is not a substitute for qualified mental health therapy.

ARE YOU A VICTIM OF OVERWHELM?

Do you ever get frustrated because:

- You can't get stuff done.
- You're perceived as lazy, or with a lack of willpower or focus.
- You have feelings of depression, helplessness, or worthlessness.
- You ask yourself, "What is wrong with me?"
- You spend too much time in your head thinking about the same task.
- You have low self-esteem.
- You can't seem to follow through.
- You are distracted by "bright, shiny objects."
- You suffer stress, lack of sleep, or other health issues.
- You repeatedly put tasks off.
- You are a perfectionist.
- When a task is large or complex, you have trouble starting it.
- You're afraid to fail (or succeed).

If you have more than a few of these feelings, you might be suffering from overwhelm. I want to be very clear. I am trained in the law and in life. I am not a psychiatrist, a psychologist, or another mental health professional. If you suffer from serious anxiety, depression, or another condition, and it persists, please see a psychological professional. I have had decades of experience in dealing with people and life, but do not treat mental illness. Please seek professional help if you or your family thinks your condition is serious or persists. Although I might not know you personally, there are several things I do know about you:

- You are not alone.
- You are not lazy.
- You are not consciously choosing to fail to complete tasks.
- You are not unmotivated.
- You can stop beating yourself up any time you want to.
- You can choose to change your situation.
- You don't have to do it alone.
- It's okay to ask for help – it's not a reflection on you as a person.
- Overwhelm can't be eliminated, but you can manage it.
- Just because it's always been this way in the past does not mean it has to be this way in the future.

CHARACTERISTICS OF HAPPY, PRODUCTIVE PEOPLE

Some people are born happy and productive. Bitches! There are certain traits they have naturally, while the rest of us must learn them:

- Clarity of vision
- Precise goals
- Follow-through on commitments
- Willingness to tackle the big stuff
- Reliability
- Focus

PLANNING

Happy, productive people also know that failing to plan is planning to fail. This applies to everything. You need a plan that will help you:

- Determine your big "why."
- Set goals so you know which elephant to eat.
- Find out what you want the outcome to be.
- Approach a challenge.
- Decide which part of your elephant to eat first.

Perhaps just reading that list generates feelings of overwhelm, and that's okay as long as you realize that there is a way to overcome those feelings. The benefits of completing the program laid out in *Eat the Elephant* are wide-ranging. Some include:

- Increased productivity
- Stronger self-esteem
- Completion of tasks
- Feelings of freedom
- Self-confidence
- A positive outlook on life
- A clear vision of what you want your life to look like
- More satisfying relationships

"Okay, that sounds good," you say. "But I'm so busy; I don't have time to take on one more project."

How much time do you spend thinking about how much you have to do or what you haven't yet done? If you could cut your thinking-about-it time by 20 percent, what would that be worth to you? What if you could cut it by 30 percent, or 50 percent, or even more? Once you are clear about where you want to go and how you want to get there, you will find time to... oh, I don't know, maybe have some fun! You do remember what that is, right? You might have time to read a book for pleasure, or even take a vacation. Mmmmm.

You've already made the financial investment of buying this book, which is negligible compared to the value you're getting, so money is not an issue. But I hear you saying, "I don't have any experience with this sort of thing, and what if it's all that woo-woo stuff? I'll pass." Frankly, if that's your internal dialog, that could be one reason you're stuck and overwhelmed. Whether you realize it or not, you have been choosing to stay where you are and suffer rather than taking action to have a better life. In order to change your circumstances, *you* have to change – not radical change; a slight change in perspective or outlook can make a huge difference.

Experience and objectivity are my gifts to you. There are millions of people just like you who have the same anxieties and fears. By acknowledging that, you have already taken the first step to overcoming overwhelm. I have helped hundreds of people alter their perspectives to achieve great success and happiness. And I can help you, too, as long as you are willing to put forth the effort. You can't phone this in. Do the exercises to get the results.

It is easier to see someone else's bumps in the jungle than it is to see your own. While I've seen overwhelm issues in others and can identify them, my own stuff takes a lot more effort. It's easy to be objective about others, but not so much about yourself. Until you've eaten the elephant in your own life, you can't possibly know how difficult, frustrating, painful, annoying – choose your own adjective – it really is. Until you've walked the walk, you can't credibly talk the talk.

I am offering you the chance to make a choice. You have the power to choose how you want to live the rest of your life.

Choose wisely.

YOUR ELEPHANT

The first thing to do is decide what your elephant is. For some it's starting from square one and asking yourself what you want your life to look like. For those who already have an idea about what they want from life, doing the exercises in *Eat the Elephant* can provide greater clarity.

Be willing to say yes to opportunities; "just say no" guarantees that you will continue to be mired in overwhelm. Only by saying yes can you change your circumstances. Be willing to:

- Move forward even when the path isn't clear.
- Bring your light into the world in a big way.
- Pursue your goals even when they scare you shitless.
- Take the first step even if you don't know the whole "how."

Success is hanging in there long after others let go. You can't *think* your way to success; you must *work* your way to success. In order to succeed:

- Stop playing the blame game with yourself and others.

- Ask for help. Friends, colleagues, and social media might have suggestions for specific actions you can take toward eating your elephant.

- Remember that you are not alone, lazy, worthless, or a bad person.

- Stop thinking about the problem for a while and let your subconscious take over. You can tap in to your own inspiration, encouragement, and creativity.

- HAVE A PLAN! Having a plan rooted in your values and goals provides a map of where you want to go and how to get there.

We all carry within us the seeds of self-sabotage. It takes more than just having a positive attitude and feeling good about yourself to overcome those pesky buggers. Be brutally honest about how you sabotage yourself, even when it is uncomfortable. Growth and change are not comfortable. In fact, sometimes they can be downright torture. But knowing that growth will come out of this process should encourage you to continue. Be willing to embrace both the positives and negatives of growth. Being open to new ideas and new ways of doing things will help break down your natural tendency to resist change.

Be patient with yourself. You are a mere mortal, but with vast potential. Rome wasn't built in a day, and neither will you overcome overwhelm overnight. Overcoming overwhelm is not for wimps, but you are no wimp!

Q: *How can you tell when there's been an elephant in the refrigerator?*

A: *Footprints in the butter.*

3 DEFINING WHO YOU ARE

"Happiness is that state of consciousness which proceeds from the achievement of one's values."

—Ayn Rand

In order to decide what to pay attention to and what you can ignore, know what your values are. Values are the qualities you hold as important to the way you live and work. They are the yardsticks you use, often subconsciously, to determine whether your life is turning out the way you want it to. Your core values (such as honesty, integrity, work ethic, etc.) remain largely unchanged throughout your adult life, but you adjust them as time and circumstances change. If you are not certain of your core values, or need a refresher, try the exercise below. Write your answers down so you can experience both the intellectual and visual results of your work.

1. When were you the happiest in your personal or professional life? What was happening? What were you doing? Were you alone or with others? Where were you?

2. When were you most proud of yourself? Did you do something? Did you not do something? Were other people proud of you or was it internal pride?

3. When were you the most satisfied and content? What desire was fulfilled? Was there an experience that had special meaning? How? Why?

4. Look at your answers to numbers 1, 2, and 3 above. What do they have in common? Are there certain internal or external factors that resonate with you? Are there any that can be combined into one core value? Write down what seem to be your ten top values based on your answers. Use the following list to help you get started, and feel free to add your own ideas.

Accountability	Boldness
Accuracy	Calmness
Achievement	Carefulness
Adventurousness	Challenge
Altruism	Cheerfulness
Ambition	Clear-minded
Assertiveness	Commitment
Balance	Community
Being the best	Compassion
Belonging	Competitiveness

Consistency

Contentment

Continuous growth

Contribution

Control

Cooperation

Correctness

Courtesy

Creativity

Curiosity

Decisiveness

Dependability

Determination

Devoutness

Diligence

Discipline

Discretion

Diversity

Dynamism

Economy

Effectiveness

Efficiency

Elegance

Empathy

Enjoyment

Enthusiasm

Equality

Excellence

Excitement

Expertise

Exploration

Expressiveness

Fairness

Faith

Family

Fidelity

Fitness

Fluency

Focus

Freedom

Fun

Generosity

Goodness

Grace

Growth

Happiness

Hard work

Health

Helping

Holiness

Honesty	Piety
Honor	Positivity
Humility	Practicality
Independence	Preparedness
Ingenuity	Professionalism
Inner harmony	Prudence
Inquisitiveness	Quality
Insightfulness	Reliability
Integrity	Resourcefulness
Intelligence	Restraint
Intuition	Results
Joy	Rigor
Justice	Security
Leadership	Self-knowledge
Legacy	Self-control
Love	Selflessness
Loyalty	Self-reliance
Mastery	Sensitivity
Merit	Serenity
Obedience	Service
Openness	Shrewdness
Order	Simplicity
Originality	Soundness
Patriotism	Speed
Perfection	Spontaneity

Stability	Timeliness
Strategic	Tolerance
Strength	Traditionalism
Structure	Truth-seeker
Success	Understanding
Support	Uniqueness
Teamwork	Unity
Temperance	Usefulness
Thankfulness	Vision
Thoroughness	Vitality
Thoughtfulness	

5. Next, prioritize your list. This is often the toughest part because all the values you selected are important. But do your best to come up with the top ten. Then narrow your list to the top five. Use "progressive comparison analysis" as a guide: Write your list of ten in any order. Look at the first two items. If you could only choose one, which is more important to you? Compare that item with the next one on the list. Which of those is more important? Continue down the list until you have the one item on the list that is the most important to you. Then start over with the top item remaining on the list and do the exercise again. Continue in this way until you have eliminated all but five items, and those are your core values.

6. Study your top five list. Even if the items are slightly different from what you thought they might be at the beginning of the exercise, do they make you feel good about yourself? Would you be proud to share your values with others? Do these values represent your vision of your ideal life?

Congratulations! As I encourage you to do with all the exercises in *Eat the Elephant*, put your list away for a day or so and revisit it. Repeat step six. Are your values still a good fit with how you see your life? If so, great. If not, see if tweaking them makes you more comfortable. You can now filter out distractions that are not in accord with your values.

Q: *Why do elephants drink so much?*

A: *They're trying to forget.*

4 WHERE ARE YOU GOING?

"If you want to live a happy life, tie it to a goal, not to people or things."

—Albert Einstein

Now that you know your core values, it's time to decide where you want to go, and what you want to accomplish. You'll want a map so your inner GPS will know where to direct you, and so you'll know when you get there. Unlike the days of your youth when you could pile in a car with a bunch of friends and an 8-track player and just drive, your life is no longer spring break. Your future is serious business and deserves serious attention. A goal is a wish with a plan, but the plan is the important part.

There are many benefits of setting personal goals in addition to overcoming overwhelm, among which are:

- Allowing for the most productive use of time
- Reducing stress
- Keeping you motivated

- Giving clarity and focus to your activities
- Providing purpose
- Improving concentration and performance
- Increasing self-esteem and confidence
- Allowing for greater satisfaction and happiness

It is by design, not fiat, that goal-setting is next in this process after identifying your values. And it's the most effective step.

To set meaningful goals, visualize what you want for your life. Your vision might be to make a lot of money, to travel, to succeed in business, to be of service to others, to play professional baseball, to find the cure for cancer, or to be a good parent. Whatever your vision is, be clear about it. Take some time; try on several scenarios and see what feels right.

At this point don't worry about how you are going to accomplish your goals; we'll get to that later. For now your vision and goals are about what *you* want to *do or be*. What do you want your life to look like? Where do you want to live? Do you want to work for a big corporation or a small business, or own your own business? Do you want a spouse, life partner, children? What do you want to do for fun and recreation? Without a vision, you have no destination to plug in to your personal GPS. If you don't know where you want to go, you will never get there.

There are several ways to go about setting personal goals. I'll share the one I think works best, but feel free to alter it to suit your particular needs. I divided my life into areas of interest: family, career/professional, financial, recreation/social, creative, educational, health/well-being, spiritual, and service.

Choose categories that pertain to you at the moment, or add your own, but I encourage you to do this exercise with all areas of your life in the near future. Once you know the process of goal-setting, you can adapt it to any project or activity you want to achieve.

For this exercise let's work on the career/professional category. Get a sheet of paper and write down everything you want to achieve in your career or calling. Do not censor yourself; do not lift the pen from the page; do not think or analyze. Come hell or high water, keep writing and do not stop until you have at least forty items. Then write ten more. To help you brainstorm, ask yourself these questions:

- What do I enjoy?
- What do I do well?
- What do I want to be?
- Where do I want to go?
- What do I want to do?
- What do I want to have?

- What do I want to give?
- What do I *not* want to be, do, have, and give?

Don't rush this exercise. Give it serious thought, time, and consideration; the rest of your life depends on it. Once you have your list, put it aside and go for a walk, cook a meal, watch a movie, or take a nap. Later, or even tomorrow, review your list, and if any items seem too farfetched, draw a single line through them. You wrote them down for a reason, so don't obliterate them because you might want to revisit them later.

Next, group like items together, such as things you like in one list and things you don't like in another. Sometimes the things you don't want are strangely more illuminating that those you do. Add more ideas as they come to you.

Decide which goals are long term – five, ten, twenty years out – and which are short term – to be completed within the next year. Then settle on the mid-range goals, which you will complete in one to five years. Within the lists of similar goals you created above, create three lists of short-term, mid-range, and long-term goals.

Now pick one goal that you can start on now. You will set more goals as you go, but in the interest of avoiding overwhelm, start with one. Think carefully with both your head and your heart when choosing your goal. Try it on for size and see how it feels. Are you satisfied? If so, good. If not, repeat the exercise until you are sure you can live with your choice – because you will.

Now you will make it a "SMART" goal, which is a concept originally used in business planning, but that works just as well when setting personal goals. Although people differ on exactly what the letters stand for, generally a S.M.A.R.T. goal is: specific, measureable, attainable, relevant, and time-bound.

To illustrate the SMART method, let's use an example: Say your goal is to be a millionaire so you can set up a foundation to provide scholarships for children of military personnel killed in the line of duty. It's *specific*, not vague or general.

Goals must be *measurable.* Being a millionaire is easily measureable by looking at a bank or brokerage statement, so you're set there.

Goals must be *attainable*. Just as hope is not a strategy, buying lottery tickets is not retirement planning. While your goal should be a stretch, it should not be the impossible dream.

Goals must be *relevant*. Skydiving might be something you want to try, but it is not a goal because it will not move you toward your goal of becoming a millionaire or providing the scholarships. (The former trial lawyer in me anticipates an objection. If you have a terrible accident while skydiving and become paralyzed, and you sue the parachute company and get a $1 million verdict, you will be a millionaire for a fleeting moment. Then the lawyer will have their hand out, the court will want its costs, and medical providers will want their bills paid. You will have what's left, but you're in a wheelchair and you still don't have $1 million, so that plan sucks.)

Goals must be *time-bound*. Set a deadline for becoming a millionaire that is realistic, but firm.

For our millionaire example, the SMART goal might be: "I will have $1 million in my investment account in ten years doing [whatever work you choose]. I will earn $150,000 each year adjusted for inflation." Or you might set a graduated scale of increasing income over the ten years, such as $100,000 the first year, $150,000 the second, $225,000 the third, etc. Yes, $150,000 per year for ten years is $1.5 million, but unless you adopt a homeless, care-less, food-less, fun-less existence, you'll need walking-around money, and the tax man always has his hands in your pocket.

This example is specific (have $1 million), measurable ($150,000 per year), attainable (only you will know that, so be realistic), relevant (again, only you will know the relevance), and time-bound (ten years). Notice that you have identified the "what," but not the "how." Fear not, you will get to the "how."

Write down your goal! Having it swirling around in your head is a surefire recipe for both remaining stuck in overwhelm and not accomplishing your goal. Write your goal as a positive statement in the present tense. For example, "I will be a millionaire on _____ [ten years from today's date]."

Goals and your progress thereon should be reevaluated regularly. I review my goals quarterly, and at that time plan for the next ninety days. When reviewing your goals, ask yourself how you did. If you completed the goal too easily, you're playing too small and need to make the next quarter's goal more of a stretch. If you did not achieve your goal, you might have underestimated the scope of the project or overestimated your efficiency. Identify the roadblocks that got in the way, and reevaluate the timeline for your goal.

Q: *Where do you find elephants?*

A: *It depends on where you lost them.*

5 SABOTEURS

"By prevailing over all obstacles and distractions, one may unfailingly arrive at his chosen goal or destination."

—Christopher Columbus

The overwhelm sea is rife with pirates – saboteurs whose mission is to hijack you away from your goals. The sooner you can spy those lousy buccaneers the better your chance of keelhauling them and navigating safely toward port. These pirates manifest themselves as distractions. Being able to identify and eliminate them is key to overcoming overwhelm.

SQUIRREL, SQUIRREL

One distraction is "Bright Shiny Object Syndrome" (BSOS), also known as "squirrel moments." Your attention flips from one thing to another, and you can't get anything done. It isn't quite ADD or ADHD, but they share common characteristics. As you are working on a project, a new idea captures your imagination and you let it take you away from your task. When the excitement of the new idea wanes, you get another new idea, and run with that. Meanwhile the first project remains incomplete, and your goal unrealized.

Most people who suffer from BSOS are passionate, willing to take risks, and intelligent. There are so many ideas flying through their heads that focus is a problem. They also love challenges, and once they've figured out the solution to a problem they get bored with that project and seek something to generate excitement and passion again. The problem comes in the lack of discipline that accompanies BSOS.

If you are captivated by the energy and excitement that surrounds something new, you're not alone; I am, too. After the thrill and challenge of a project are over, I sometimes get bored with the rest of the work because it is no longer challenging. The result is that many things get started and few are completed. There is no cure for BSOS – it is a chronic condition. What you can do, however, is learn to recognize when you get derailed and take steps to rope yourself back into your current project. You can't white-knuckle your way through BSOS, but you can train yourself to minimize its distractions.

Meditation is wonderful training for this. My first attempts at meditation were insane. The instructor said to focus on the breath and empty my mind.

Good luck with that! My "monkey mind" is going all the time. I didn't even last for half an inhale. It was terribly frustrating even though it was supposed to reduce stress. With practice I can now sit still and meditate for a short time before I get antsy. I'm not ready for a full-day retreat (and I doubt if I could stay silent that long), but I can sit quietly with myself and not explode. And I have been able to translate that effort to my battle with BSOS. Getting control of BSOS is an important step in overcoming overwhelm.

YOUR WHY

Not knowing why you are pursuing your goals can also be a distraction. If you are unclear on your purpose, it is difficult to know what is important and what may be distractions. Why are you doing what you're doing? Do you know? Surprisingly, most people do not. This lack of curiosity is a distraction. You can know where you want to go and how you want to get there, but if you don't know *why* you're going, it's more difficult to stay on track. Your why goes to the essence of who you are, and it's the motivation that keeps you going when the going gets tough.

Simon Sinek wrote a great book titled *Start with Why,* in which he explains the importance of knowing why you choose to do what you do. The "what" and the "how" are important, but the "why" is the core of your motivation. Check out his TED talks on YouTube.

For example, service is my "why," which is why I wrote this book. When those of us in the service world find or create something of value, we share it with the world. That's what we do. Serving others is my highest and best purpose.

What's yours?

MINDSET

Your mindset can be another saboteur lurking in the darkness. In the nonscientific realm, *mindset* is how you look at your surroundings and your relationship to them. It is the context through which you experience your world. It can be positive or negative, but rarely neutral. Having a positive attitude when facing situations can be the difference between success and failure, and is always the gateway to joy.

My mother is ninety-two years old, and her default setting is negative – a glass-half-empty kinda gal. Often when I suggest another possible way to look at her annoyance du jour, she replies, "Oh, you're such a Pollyanna." While she doesn't mean it as a compliment, to me it is. I would much rather see my life through a positive lens – a kaleidoscope, if you will, of possibilities. I'm not going to change my mother's basic outlook on life at her age, but when I "talk her off the ledge" about her current conundrum, she feels better and can see how there is another way to think about her situation. She changes her mindset for a brief moment. Now that she has experienced my ruthless attempts to bring joy into her life for a while, she makes the transition more quickly and easily. At ninety-two you can't ask for more than that.

How can you change your mindset? As with most things, you first must be aware of what it is now. Are you content? Does your mindset foster the highest level of performance you have in you, and bring you joy? If so, you are very fortunate. If not, have faith, which is a component of mindset, whether it is in God, Yahweh, Mohammed, Spirit, the Universe, or another deity or non-deity of your choice. Carol Dweck, a professor at Stanford University, has researched mindset and written extensively about it. She discovered that when people are in a fixed mindset, they believe that their skills or intelligence are traits that are stagnant. However, when people have a growth mindset, they believe that their abilities and intelligence can be developed through conscientious effort and training. Mindset is a huge component of personal development. If you are interested in learning more about mindset, check out the "Resources" section at www.KarolynBlume.com.

GRATITUDE

One of the best antidotes for the oppression and distraction of overwhelm is gratitude. Being grateful for the gifts you have is a powerful boost to your psyche and helps you fend off distractions. Neuroscience has shown that by consciously acknowledging what you are grateful for, your subconscious is more positive and resilient when facing challenges.

My first step in using gratitude to fight overwhelm was to think of three things I was grateful for before I fell asleep. As time passed, that morphed into writing in a gratitude journal every night. Going to sleep with thankful thoughts of the abundance I have frees my subconscious from the challenges of the day. Think of new things to be grateful for each day. I am grateful for our fabulous daughter every minute of every day, and her name appears as the first entry on the first day of my journal, but each day I choose three different things to acknowledge. Some are from nature – a beautiful sunset; a huge, red, beefsteak tomato; the grandeur of a mountain vista; or the rolling sea. Some are kindnesses someone has done, either for me or someone else. Sometimes I recount an amusing situation that made me laugh. Sometimes I'm just grateful for getting out of bed in the morning, as there were days in my past when I wasn't able to. You can find something to be grateful for anywhere you look. So each evening write three of them in your gratitude journal. I prefer a separate journal for gratitude so I can easily reread my entries and instantly put things in perspective when times are tough.

Your entries can be very short. The nightly exercise takes less than a minute, but the effect lasts a long time. Take a minute (literally) now and write down the first three things you think of. I try to confine my entries to ten words or less each. Think of it as Twitter on steroids. During the day I often think that I must remember to put a happening in my journal.

Try this for a week and see how it feels. Sarah Ban Breathnach has written extensively about gratitude in her book *Simple Abundance*. One of my favorite quotes from her book is "When I surrendered my desire for security and sought serenity instead, I looked at my life with open eyes. I saw that I had much for which to be grateful. I felt humbled by my riches and regretted that I took for granted the abundance that already existed in my life. How could I expect more from the universe when I didn't appreciate what I already had?"

HITS AND MISSES

In most ventures there are winners and losers. I prefer the terms *successes* and *coulda-been-successes*. The difference between a success and a coulda-been is the level of commitment you make to improve your situation. Your life doesn't get better by chance, but by choice and change. If you choose to do the work to change where you are to where you want to be, you can crack the overwhelm nut. If not, you'll continue in the overwhelm rut. When you realize it doesn't always have to be this way, the landscape opens to new possibilities and ultimately freedom and joy.

By changing your perspective on your to-dos and being more selective about how and when you add items to the list, your to-dos become manageable. When you add items to the list, others should be deleted, either through completion or reprioritization, to see progress and feel the satisfaction of unburdening yourself. Your to-do elephant will become smaller and smaller before your eyes.

When a new idea or opportunity (or bright, shiny object) presents itself, ask yourself whether pursuing it would move you closer to your goal. Is it in alignment? Is it a distraction? Does it look interesting without moving you closer to your goal? What are the rewards of pursuing the new idea relative to the plan you have in place? The answers to these questions help you evaluate the costs of diverting your attention from your previous plan to pursue the new idea. When you get stuck, ask a friend, mentor, or colleague for an objective opinion. Do both projects have equal weight in moving your goals forward? Should one be discarded or deferred in favor of the other? Can you delegate some or all of one task to someone else?

To all my perfectionist friends, beware: You might even find out that sometimes good enough is good enough. For me, that was the hardest of all lessons to learn. Throughout my youth I was told that I wasn't good enough, smart enough, or talented enough. I took those messages to heart and carried them with me for decades. I never questioned whether those assessments were true; I just believed them. So I worked harder than most people, both in my personal and professional life. And no matter what I did or how hard I worked, it was never good enough for me. Rarely did I get complaints from others about my lack of effort, results, or commitment, but I constantly strove to be what I had been told was perfect.

But who decides what is good enough? Who defines perfection? What is the standard or yardstick against which perfect is measured? When I asked myself these questions, I found that the criteria I was using were subjective standards set by others, and that there is no such thing as perfect. I learned to be comfortable with the notion that as long as I put forth my best effort in integrity, generosity, and gratitude, my best was good enough. And good enough *is* good enough.

Often people feel they need to be "fixed" – preferably a quick fix that is painless and involves little work. This quest for an easy fix has resulted in a multi-billion-dollar self-help industry. But many people still suffer from overwhelm. If you are looking for a quick fix, read no further. Give this book to someone who is willing to do the work necessary to overcome overwhelm. Magic wands only work in fairy tales; for the rest of us, it takes effort.

This program is work, like anything else worthwhile. While it is simple, it is not easy. It takes time and commitment to change the way you deal with being overwhelmed. You know that the old ways don't work. A change in your outlook and the way you approach challenges is what you need. Until you change yourself, the world will not change. Or to use one of my all-time favorite sayings: If you keep doing what you're doing, you'll keep getting what you're getting.

Let's try something new.

Q: *Why do elephants have trunks?*

A: *They'd look silly with suitcases.*

6 THE PAST IS PROLOGUE

*"Every word, facial expression, gesture or action
on the part of a parent gives the child some message
about self-worth. It is sad that so many parents
don't realize what messages they are sending."*
—Virginia Satir

Feelings of being overwhelmed are most often rooted in childhood. The behaviors that feed them – busyness, fear, procrastination, perfectionism, resistance, avoidance – are not intrinsic to human nature. They are learned behaviors that result from interacting with parents, teachers, and peers, and your reactions to these people. They are thieves of your spirit. They rob you of the basic joy of life. Once you recognize them and the deleterious effect they have on your well-being, you can begin to jettison them from your emotional buffet.

By way of example, I will give you the *"Readers' Digest"* version of my story: I was born on a hot summer day in New York City when Yogi Berra was the catcher for the Yankees and bomb shelters were on every block, marked by a big black and yellow "S." We had air-raid drills in school during which we had to sit under our desks to practice for when an atomic bomb would be launched at the U.S. by the Soviet Union. It never dawned on me in first grade to ask how the desk would protect me; my penchant for questioning authority emerged much later. When Mrs. Carey said, "Under the desks," we went under the desks. It was a time of great fear, even for small children. Although I had no idea what this desk-ducking business was all about, I knew it was not a game. The grownups were constantly on edge, so I knew it must be something bad. My "spidey sense" was on guard from a very young age. The fear that I felt around me made me hyper-vigilant of my environment, which played out throughout my life. As the years went on, the drills ceased and the bombs did not fall, but "the times they were a-changin'."

As the oldest, I was expected to set an example for the other kids, which is a heavy burden to put on a little kid. By the time I was ten years old I was babysitting for my siblings on a regular basis. The thought scares the daylights out of me now. I cannot imagine having left our four-year-old daughter in the care of a ten-year-old, and I had three siblings! Being in charge was a nightmare, which is where I got the moniker "the bossy older sister," which lives on today. I began to learn the importance of negotiating, a skill I honed as a mother and a lawyer. My parents' constant scrutiny of my behavior toward the "little kids" was the beginning of my perfectionism. You'll see how this is connected *infra*. (I really needed my lawyerly Latin fix. Whew, glad that's out of my system.)

I began high school in 1966, at a time when the Viet Nam war was raging. My parents were very conservative Republicans, somewhat to the right of Attila the Hun. I, on the other hand, was a freethinking liberal – against the war, against the establishment, and for peace, love, hope, generosity, and freedom. Ah, the seeds of my early rebellion during the duck-under-the-desk days emerged with a vengeance. I saw rebellion and independent thinking as a way to make my mark in the world. Needless to say I was not a hit at home.

The peace movement was a huge part of my high school years. I worked on lowering the voting age from twenty-one to eighteen. In tenth grade I cut school with two friends to attend a rally for Eugene McCarthy in Central Park. That escapade amazes me now, but at the time I had no fear about pursuing what I knew was right and just. I learned that I – li'l ol' me – could change the world. My juices were flowing, and my passion ignited in the service of others. My vision was far bigger than myself.

I hung around with the cool kids, but I also hung around with the brainiacs, the jocks, the nerds, the preppies, and the hippies. I liked and got along with all kinds of people, an attribute that has served me well in life.

I came of age in the late 1960s, the era of free love, drugs, peace marches, and women's liberation. Although I was much too well endowed to burn my bra on the steps of a government building, I was an activist in the movement.

What chores we were assigned at home depended more on our age than our gender. My first big bump up against sex discrimination came in law school. The mid-1970s saw an increase in the number of women admitted to law schools, but the profession was still an old boys' network to its core. When I opened my law office, I was one of six women out of 300 lawyers practicing in my county. But I was undeterred, even though I was viewed as a freak by most of my colleagues. Some were intrigued, some were horrified, and some were certain that if I got married and had a family I would quit the practice of law. Clearly they did not know me.

I did, in fact, get married, and two years later we had a daughter. Those were the "women can have it all" days. There was a perfume commercial jingle that went, "I can bring home the bacon. Fry it up in a pan. And never let you forget you're a man," that stoked the fire of my relentless pursuit of unrealistic goals. What I had to discover on my own was that women (and men for that matter) can have it all, but not all at the same time. That bit of wisdom thirty-five years ago would have saved me a world of hurt. As it was, the having-it-all concept forced me into a life of relentless exhaustion, self-loathing, and frustration. I couldn't ask for help because I was supposed to be able to do it all, but I couldn't do it all. The harder I tried, the more frustrated and less fulfilled I felt, and asking for help was a sign of weakness or failure. If I only worked harder, I could live up to the unreasonable standards the media presented. UGH!

There was always more to do, both on the home front and the work front. I wanted to be a good mother, wife, lawyer, and citizen of the world. My family was and is the most important thing in my life. I also had to prove myself in the courtroom by working harder and longer than my male counterparts. And I am a perfectionist, which made my efforts in both arenas lacking. While my intuition told me something was very wrong with the way I was living my life, my head relentlessly instructed me to suck it up and work harder. There had to be something wrong with me if I couldn't cut it. I showed up and did my job, took care of my family, volunteered at school, and sat on several non-profit boards. I kept on going despite my depleting reserves of energy and enthusiasm. What I didn't realize at the time was that most women in my situation felt the same way, but we were either embarrassed about it or afraid to admit it.

Looking back I can see that my perfectionism and susceptibility to overwhelm began when I was born. My father, a functional alcoholic, could not be satisfied by anyone or anything. Throughout his life not only was I never good enough, never smart enough, never capable enough – never enough, but no one and nothing else was either. The environment he created was mired in negativity and criticism. Never were the positive aspects of a person or situation discussed or acknowledged – only what was wrong or lacking. I never felt loved or cherished or respected. Often I felt like gum on the bottom of his shoe. I thought that if I worked harder, I would no longer be a disappointment to him. I kept trying, even after I realized it was futile. In the spring semester of my junior year in college, I got a 4.0 grade point average. When my father saw my report card, his response was, "But two of them are A-minuses." I was crushed to my core, and for about a year he and I had no contact.

Can you imagine what's coming? After I was admitted to law school, my father offered to send me to secretarial school if I would give up the ridiculous idea of becoming a lawyer. Needless to say I declined his offer. But all too often the eyes of a critical parent become the lens through which you see yourself and your place in the world.

Those feelings of inadequacy followed me for decades, into middle age. Even though I had achieved great professional and personal success, had a great daughter and husband, had many friends, and enjoyed participating in charitable activities, I could not shake my feelings of overwhelm because it was never good enough, at least in my eyes. I became a "human doing" rather than a human being. There was always more to do, and when I wasn't doing something, I felt guilty, which gave fuel to my lack of self-esteem and overwhelm.

As the years went by, I became more and more depressed, not just cocktail-party-conversation depressed, but clinically depressed. My get up and go got up and went. I found it more and more difficult to complete tasks and achieve goals. For several years I floundered, absolutely rudderless, which I covered up so well that my suffering was largely unnoticed by family and friends. But I knew deep down that I was failing at life because I couldn't accomplish what I set out to do. I had no energy, no enthusiasm, no joy. The only thing I felt was pain, and I was sinking deeper and deeper into the dark hole of self-loathing. Why couldn't I get something, anything, done; why wouldn't the pain stop? I was overwhelmed by the simplest of chores. The dishwasher would sit full and clean for days because I just couldn't bring myself to unload it, and I am not a lazy person.

In the midst of my misery, something in me shifted, and I realized that, the Universe willing, I would have another thirty years or so on this planet. I asked myself, "Do I always want to feel this way?" The answer was a resounding no, so I set about looking at what I was really doing and why I was doing those things. Who was I and did I like that person?

After years of medication and counseling, I was able to look at my life more objectively. A huge eureka moment occurred when I realized that my father's dissatisfaction with me had very little to do with me and very much to do with him. He was a very unhappy soul, and nothing anyone did changed that. I was not responsible for his misery and I couldn't let his unhappiness continue to be my own. Since he was not one for self-reflection or introspection on any level, conversations were pointless. He disdained any semblance of a spiritual or heart-centered life, which was antithetical to my very spiritual and heart-centered outlook. By the end of his life, I had made peace and agreed to disagree.

As I learned more about myself, I discovered that I have many gifts that I had shared with my clients over the years. People have always come to me for advice, and I have been referred to as "the voice of reason." Some of my most valuable gifts are my perception, empathy, compassion, instinct, and sense of humor. My clients appreciate my down-to-earth practical focus and my ability to quickly see what the problem is and create a system that helps resolve their issue with a minimum of angst. (Notice I said "a minimum of angst," not "angst-free." If it were easy and painless, everybody would solve their problems angst-free.) I have helped clients get their mojo back when they had no idea how to do it, or even that they needed to. So why couldn't I do the same thing for myself? That became my big "why" – to learn to conquer my overwhelm and depression, and discover true joy.

In order to eat my own elephant, I engaged in self-reflection, journaling, coaching, training, counseling, medication, and more shelf-help than you can imagine (you know, those products you buy to fix you, but they sit on the shelf and do nothing). I spent years studying theories of happiness, productivity, neuroscience, psychology, and spirituality. But there were no prescriptions to help me get out of my state of total despair. No one had it neatly packaged in a "how to right what's wrong" program, and I knew I was not the only one who suffered debilitating overwhelm. It was then that I decided I had to create the solution I was looking for. My mission became clear: I had to synthesize all of the information I had collected in my vast experience with people, research, and introspection and create a program to help me burst out from my prison of overwhelm.

When I was free of the incessant self-loathing and negative self-talk, I reevaluated all aspects of my life. After practicing law for twenty-five years, I realized that slamming one another around a courtroom is no way to resolve disputes. Until then I hadn't fully realized the toxic culture of the practice of law. I knew there had to be a better way to resolve conflicts, and I discovered mediation (not meditation, mediation). For ten years I mediated all types of cases both here and abroad. Through the several hundred cases I mediated and facilitated, I came to know that all conflict begins internally. Whether it's the conflict in the Middle East or the neighbor's barking dog, it comes from how you see the world and your place in it. I now spend my professional time helping people get unstuck, address their inner self-talk, and overcome overwhelm.

This eureka moment took several years, lots of trial and error, and lots of failed plans, but what came from my work is *Eat the Elephant*. I didn't come into this world to get anything; my mission is to give, whether it's compassion, expertise, comfort, knowledge, guidance, or whatever else is needed. My mantra since high school has been "doing well by doing good." These core values continue to guide my life: service, integrity, and excellence. I believe the only person I can count on 100 percent of the time to have my best interests at heart is me, so I follow my intuition.

I now appreciate the importance of integrating the intellectual and practical aspects of life (read:

head and heart) in order to live a full and happy life, something that eluded me in my younger years. The greatest gift I can share with you is to guide your moving beyond the limitations you consciously or unconsciously impose on yourself. Through my decades of experience and perspective, which bring intellectual study and research together with practical, real-life experience and knowledge, I help people get unstuck and move forward in the direction of their dreams. You can zero in on your stumbling blocks using this concise program. You will see results.

I ate my elephant by working through many layers to create a life that is both successful and satisfying. The Eat-the-Elephant program helped me, and it will help you, too.

Q: *Where do elephants with skin problems go?*

A: *Pachydermatologists.*

7 WHIRLING DERVISH

"I'm late, I'm late for a very important date. No time to say hello. Goodbye. I'm late, I'm late, I'm late."
—the white rabbit, Walt Disney's *Alice in Wonderland*

Do you feel as if you're always rushing around, but not getting anything done? Are you always in action, but at the end of the day you don't feel you've accomplished anything of note? Many people think they must always be busy – so much to do, so little time. Our culture reinforces this by bombarding us with messages that sound urgent or like a once-in-a-lifetime opportunity: "Act now to avoid missing the chance"; "One-time only offer"; "This price will expire without notice"; "Limited time only." You want to avoid disappointment, so everything takes on the urgency of whoever or whatever is delivering the message. Others tell you, "If you put your mind to it, you can do anything." What a crock!

Somewhere along the line, society got the idea that you must be busy, work faster, and multitask more to get ahead in business and in life. Putting in the longest hours, the most weekends, and being on call 24/7 are perceived to be the keys to success. But there is a difference between working on your business and working on your busyness. The same is true for living your life and being a slave to busyness.

Some people believe that being busy all the time allows others, often those in positions of authority, to see them as smart, competent, and important. Busyness has become not just a way of life, but a badge of honor. People compete to be the busiest. If you are in such demand that you are busy all the time, you must be very good at what you do. But what are you good at – getting stuff done or being busy with nonsense? Who are you important to – others or yourself? It should be noted that when you multitask, none of the tasks you are doing are being done well. The brain cannot give full attention to multiple tasks at the same time.

There are a plethora of people who are full of ideas for how you should spend your time or live your life. Parents are good at doling out unsolicited advice, as are friends and colleagues. Family, friends, colleagues, and the media all have ideas on what you should do. Frankly, I don't like people "shoulding" all over me. Advice is fine if it is meant in a constructive way, but there is a fine line between wise counsel and manipulation or bossiness.

Just as people think they can solve your problems, they choose the easy way out and focus on your issues rather than their own. It is always easier to give advice than to take it, or figure it out for yourself. Most of these Dear Abby types are well intentioned, but may have an agenda. And that agenda may or may not be the same as yours. Their agenda won't serve your interests above all others. This is where clarity on what you want your life to look like is important. It is always easier to tell others how to live their lives than it is to create and live your own, but whose life do you want to live – yours or someone else's?

Let's find out which activities contribute to your busyness. For one week keep track of all of the activities that intrude on your daily schedule. List the time of day, the activity, and the amount of time spent. Do this each and every time your planned schedule is derailed, whether for a good reason or not. It is important to write down the "time vampires" as they happen. If not, you will either forget them, minimize them, or get frustrated and quit the whole exercise. Knowing what is keeping you on the busyness treadmill is crucial to figuring out how to get off.

At the end of the week, study your list. Is there a particular type of interruption that intrudes more than others? Are there times of day when your schedule is more likely to be derailed? Is there a pattern to the kinds of activities that crop up during the day and need attention? At work is there a person or activity that feeds your tendency toward busyness? Cogitate on your list for a while. What is it telling you?

Now sort your list, grouping like items together. Are there "domestic diva" duties that can be grouped together and done at the same time – cleaning, gardening, cooking, laundry? Can errands be combined into one or two trips, which would not only save time, but gas as well? Perhaps you could rearrange your office or workspace to be more conducive to efficiency and flow.

COMPLICATIONS

Clutter is a complication. Having too much stuff vying for your physical and psychological attention can zap your focus and propel you toward scattered activity, which results in busyness. Can you get rid of your extra stuff in at least one area of your home or office so you can focus on what you want to do with fewer visual distractions? Experiment. See what feels good to you and fits into your lifestyle. Then commit to that plan and try it without excuses or deviation for one week. How did you do? Was it easier to stay focused? If so, good for you. If not, where were your pitfalls? Were there tasks you hadn't thought of that got in your way? How could you tweak your plan to make it easier to follow? Keep testing until you find the one that works best for you. Then stick to it!

Like you, I am challenged by complications. Sometimes I am exhausted by the end of the day, and look back on my list of accomplishments only to find very little there. How depressing! As time goes by,

I have fewer of those days because I plan my tasks better. I pick three work-related items to complete each day and put them in order of importance based on deadlines, income-generating activity, business development and marketing, scheduled appointments with clients, etc. I make sure to do those three activities first (or as scheduled) as they are the most important for that day. Then I plan in non-essential work, personal tasks, and things that are important but not as time sensitive. For example, laundry is usually not time sensitive (though when I've put it off so long that there is no clean underwear, laundry bounces to the top of the list). Usually I cook several dishes one day per weekend so that during the week I only have to prepare vegetables to have meals ready to go. I freeze dishes for later use, especially things like soups, stews, spaghetti sauce, and casseroles. I go to the big grocery store once a month and supplement with fresh produce at local farmers' markets or smaller stores. With a little advance planning, you can reduce the time you spend on busyness by half or more.

In my business I do the same thing. I read and answer emails twice per day – in the middle and at the end of the day. Some people advise that this is a poor business strategy, but I choose to be an actor rather than a reactor in my business. When you begin your day by reading emails, you have allowed the senders and their concerns to take control of your day. You have given their agendas priority over yours. How many times have you sat down at your desk with your to-do list and great intentions to get everything done, only to open an email and have your plans derailed by someone else's crisis? At times fires do have to be put out, but not everything in your inbox is a fire. When you get such an email, don't just react. Take a minute or several to evaluate what is the real issue and what is the best way to respond, if at all. Make sure that whatever comes up is a crisis in *your* eyes, not just in someone else's. Don't be afraid to set boundaries around your time. Know what you must accomplish each day and focus on those things. By not reading my emails until noon, I ensure that I will get a few hours of work done on what I think is important before the floodgates open.

My life's mission is compassionate service, and I strive for that every day. But I've learned (sometimes the hard way) that I cannot help everyone who asks. I have to evaluate where I can be the most help, and pursue those opportunities. Other requests might be just as valid, but in order to do what I do, I cannot react to every one. Those I have neither the time nor expertise to help with, I refer to others. Sometimes the most compassionate and supportive thing you can do for someone is to be an objective resource for them and not get swept into their drama. This benefits both of you in the long run.

Families are a constant source of drama. Everybody wants your attention *right now.* Someone is always having a crisis and needs you pronto. It could be unrequited love, dissatisfaction with a job, money problems, legal issues, substance abuse, adults who behave like teenagers, or whatever. They want your sympathy, advice, intervention, attention, and for you to fix it. The key to your sanity is to decide which issues are deserving of your attention and which are just drama.

A client was frustrated because she was working all the time but wasn't getting anything done. It was having a deleterious effect on both her personal and professional life. She is a kind-hearted soul and would go out of her way to help anyone in need. What she didn't recognize was that she was expending energy on everyone else's dramas while neglecting her own needs and goals. We discussed personal boundaries and how to allocate her time and energy so that she could get her work done and enjoy her personal life while supporting her desire to help others. With the right strategy she was able to avoid being drawn into others' dramas. She also learned that she could say yes to the *person*, but no to the *task*, by explaining her time constraints. (I am reminded, however, that "no" is a complete sentence).

SOMETIMES LIFE GETS IN THE WAY

Your plan has to be flexible enough to allow for the stuff that just comes up. Life has a way of disrupting the best-laid plans. Don't beat yourself up if you can't stick to your plan every day. When you've had a miserable day, look at where life (or you, or someone else) got in your way.

Do you need to alter your plan? This is a journey, not a destination. Flexibility is your friend. If a parent, child, or close friend has a medical emergency, you need to be flexible enough to deal with the added demands on your time. Be kind to yourself; don't try to muscle through it.

Busyness is just that – busyness. It is not productive. It is not gratifying. It does not feed your soul or benefit the world. It is a distraction from those things you hold dear such as family, friends, fun, and career. I am not advocating that you follow your heart's desire while letting the garbage pile up until you can't open the door. I'm saying that you can allocate a certain amount of time to do activities such as domestic tasks, helping with homework, gardening, carpooling, going to the gym, etc. Build those things into your calendar. You can allocate a certain amount of time per day or an average amount of time per week, but set a limit on the activities that comprise the bulk of your busyness.

Q: *What is beautiful, gray, and wears glass slippers?*

A: *Cinderelephant.*

8 *HELP, I'VE FALLEN*

"I don't think that you can let the storms of life overwhelm you. When you do that, you are no better than the craziness that caused you to be under attack."
—T. D. Jakes

What is it that makes us think we have to be doing something every moment of every day? There are people who even listen to subliminal training audios while they sleep. So what's up with that?

Overcoming overwhelm is *not* a time management issue. We all have the same twenty-four hours in a day. No matter how many new day-planning systems and productivity tools you buy, there are still only twenty-four hours in a day. No more. No less. (For those perfectionists whom I'll discuss later, it is true that when daylight savings time begins and ends, there are technically twenty-three and twenty-five hours, respectively, in those two days.) If overwhelm is not a time management issue, what is the source of this craziness?

Overwhelm is the result of messy thoughts, not messy circumstances. When too many things are rolling around in your head battling for your attention, nothing is clear. It is a jumble of equal tasks jockeying for position. Imagine the New York subway at rush hour. That's what your brain is like on overwhelm. It's not a filing cabinet, it's a highly evolved thinking machine, and it needs room to think. Neuroscience has shown that you can only keep five to seven things in your conscious mind at one time. When fifty thoughts are battling for the same seven spots, it's like the rush for admission to a top university. Just as some very qualified applicants get passed over, some of your excellent ideas get lost in the chaos of your cluttered mind, and heaven forbid one of those ideas disappears from your internal radar. The fear of losing an idea causes anxiety, which adds to being overwhelmed. Organizing this mess is the lynchpin to overcoming overwhelm.

Please do the following exercise the old fashioned way, by writing it down rather than typing on an electronic device. The physical act of writing establishes a brain-hand connection that makes the result stick.

Take a fresh pad of paper (or your journal – not an old scratch pad) and a pen to a quiet place where you will be free from distractions for as long as you need to be. Write down everything – and I do mean everything – that is rolling around in your head. Do a complete brain dump. Do not censor yourself or limit the list to what you think is significant. Now is not the time to judge what is important and what is not; that comes later. Don't limit yourself – no one will see this but you. Don't stop until you have at least fifty things. The more you can get out of your head and onto paper the better, so if you can write one hundred things, go for it.

Now go get your favorite beverage, go for a walk, or do some other activity that does not involve thinking. Give your brain a rest; it has worked hard. Several hours later, or tomorrow, revisit your list – not with judgment, but to add any items that surfaced during your downtime. Write down any new information on your brain dump list. By now your spirits have improved. The weight of all those to-dos has been removed from the device between your shoulders. Relish the feeling; it will become the new normal.

For the next step in the exercise you will need a new box of crayons. Not the 8-pack, but at least the 24-pack. I am partial to the 64-pack with the built-in sharpener. Open it and take a whiff. When you feast your eyes on the many gorgeous colors, you can't help but feel good. If you are not a crayon person, choose colored markers or pencils. Again, don't be skimpy on the number of colors, and don't rummage through your junk drawers to cobble together an assortment of leftover pens from the last conference you attended. This is a valuable exercise and it deserves its own set of crayons or markers.

Take your list and your multicolored writing implements back to that quiet place where you will not be disturbed. Choose your least-favorite color and draw a line through five items that are unnecessary or irrelevant to your life, or simply don't support the goals you have established. Fear not; you can keep the list, so the ideas won't be lost. But they are not part of your current agenda. Now take your favorite color (I'm a purple girl) and put a check next to the five most important things on your list. Limit yourself to no more than five – not a single idea more – and no fair combining two or three to make one. Five is the limit (and I'm being generous, because I usually limit it to three).

The point is not to end up with a to-do list; taking out the trash should not be among the top five items. It's an inventory of what's important to you and where you want to focus your attention. You will realize that some things on your list are more complex than others. For example, writing your blog post does not have the same gravitas that writing your book does, though it is typically more time sensitive. Your five top things might take a year or more to complete. Continue to triage your list, working from either the most important to least, or vice versa, choosing colors that reflect the value of your choices. Again, no more than five items per color.

I can feel you getting antsy about the items not in the top five. Fear not! Your next step is to create a parking lot where you will park all of the ideas that you love but that are not in the top five. My parking lot is a white board on the wall of my office, but you can use a file folder, Post-it notes in strategic places, a notebook, index cards, or whatever you're comfortable with. (See, I told you all of your ideas would be safe!) Nothing is lost except the chaos. It's all there whenever you want to read it, reevaluate it, change an item's position on the list, or just fondle it.

Sit with your list as you read the next few chapters of *Eat the Elephant*. You will think of other things you want on the list as you go through the exercises. The clarity that you have just discovered will lead you to ideas gone wild and an adrenaline rush of thoughts. Go with them. Relish them. Now that the clutter is out of your head, the good stuff will emerge. But remember, no more than five items in each color.

THE CONCEPT OF OVERWHELM

In addition to messy thoughts, what are other symptoms of overwhelm? Why is it such a pervasive problem? The noise of life can be deafening. You are expected to be connected 24/7: days, nights, weekends, holidays, vacations. Always. When CNN broadcast the first Gulf War live in 1990, it was remarkable to see the bombs falling in real time. And there was the white Bronco in the OJ Simpson car chase, which was brought to televisions around the world as it was happening;

viewers couldn't turn away. Now events are broadcast live all the time. There are people who have their televisions or computers on constantly just in case something happens. Do you really want one of the seven things in your conscious mind to be somebody else's idea of what's important? Me neither.

Overwhelm can also be an excuse for inaction. You can't get a certain task done because you are too overwhelmed; at least that's what you tell yourself and others: "I'm really sorry; I just couldn't get it done. I had so much else to do and I was so overwhelmed." But inaction is a cause of overwhelm, not a symptom. (It can sound like the chicken and egg conundrum.) More often than not your inability to get something done is the result of poor planning rather than having too much to do. When faced with a big job, do you think the problem to death, or charge into the work? When the due date approaches, are you in a mad scramble to get 'er done? Do you focus on that one project and push everything else to the back burner? Think about how great it would feel to approach a big project with enthusiasm instead, thinking of novel ways to accomplish it and coming up with a brilliant plan.

For some people, as we discussed above in relation to busyness, overwhelm is a status symbol – a badge of honor or worth. In fact, overwhelm can serve as a drug for an out-of-control ego. Creating the illusion of self-worth by engaging in busyness for the sake of busyness is a waste of time and energy, and your true self knows it. You can fool all of the people some of the time, and some of the people all of the time, but you can't fool your inner truth. This attempt by the ego to derail your soul's purpose takes a toll on your spirit.

Some people don't know where to start when there is a project to accomplish, and they don't want to ask anyone for help or direction for fear of looking stupid or incompetent. This can result from a lack of clarity on the part of the person in charge of the project; perhaps the instructions are so unclear that there is no way to figure out the ultimate goal of the project. We often assume that if we don't understand, it's our fault, not a lack of communication on someone else's part. Keep asking questions until the goal and the process are clear. A side benefit of this tactic is that it forces the boss to get really clear about what they want.

Another symptom of overwhelm is to see a problem like a deer in the headlights when faced with a task that appears so huge that you haven't a clue where to start. Examples of huge challenges are losing one hundred pounds, getting into college, finding a job, and writing a book. The mere thought of losing one hundred pounds is so daunting that you just want to eat cookies, lots of cookies, and say, "Why bother? It's just too much. I'll never be able to do that." So you don't. This is when learning to eat the elephant is invaluable.

Lest you think I'm blowing smoke, over the past couple of years I've lost nearly one hundred pounds and counting, and it was work, let me tell you. Those skinny minis who preach "move more, eat less" are clueless as to what it takes. And as ironic as it sounds, I lost the weight by eating the elephant. Before you Google the Eat the Elephant Diet, it does not exist, which is a good thing since my local grocery does not feature elephant. But the concept of losing weight is the same as for any project that seems overwhelming. Here's the jewel: Chunk it down into manageable pieces and eat each piece one at a time. See, I told you it was simple, and it is. But don't let the simplicity of the solution lull you into a false sense of security. While it is simple, it is most definitely not easy. Eating the elephant takes work and commitment on your part. Instead of looking at losing one hundred pounds, I chunked it down into losing five pounds per month, which is doable, and in those months when I lost more, it was a bonus. But the plan is the same – it works for almost all goals.

The concept of overwhelm can be difficult to understand, even for those who want to. Several years ago I was in an advanced business-coaching program that was highly recommended. The coach had been in business for several years and had grossed $1 million a year. I got some good business advice, but during one of our quarterly coaching calls, I revealed that I was so overwhelmed by the number and scope of the marketing tasks on my to-do list that I had no idea which to do first. This was a huge admission for me. It isn't generally in my nature to cry "uncle" or even ask for help. The coach replied, "From now on I forbid you to use the word *overwhelm*." At first I was stunned. Then I was pissed. Not much coaching there. To think that not using the word *overwhelm* would make the feeling go away was as ignorant as thinking that ignoring the sunlight will make it night. If you don't want to call it overwhelm, call it flapergik, but the feelings are still there; the frustrations are the same. Needless to say I fired the coach, but I still had to deal with the overwhelm. You can't wish or ignore your way out of overwhelm.

FOCUS

Focus is the name of the game. Focus on what you want to accomplish. Having a hundred ideas rolling around in your head is not going to help. The brain is a thinking device, not a storage device. When you get ideas, write them down and save them in such a way that you can find them when you need them. When you get ten ideas for blog posts, product development, speaker topics, or interesting quotes, pick three, and put the rest in your "parking lot" or your "someday list." That's a good system for getting some ideas out of your head so that you don't feel so overwhelmed and don't force yourself into procrastination.

Focus, determination, and commitment differentiate the great from the near great, with focus being the key. When Derek Jeter steps up to the plate, you can see through the TV screen how single-mindedly he is focused on the pitches thrown. When James Levine conducts the Metropolitan Opera Orchestra, or Annie Lebowitz looks through the viewfinder of a camera, or Martin Scorcese directs an actor getting whacked, or Daniel Day Lewis plays Lincoln, fireworks could go off next to them and they wouldn't notice; their attention is that focused. They tune out all distractions and concentrate only on the task at hand. Alas, I don't have that kind of focus, and my guess is that you don't either. I gracefully accept my limitations, but not the state of chaos that lack of focus engenders. You can learn to recognize when you need to hone your focus and move toward your goals with strength of purpose. Stay tuned.

Q: *What do you do with an elephant with three balls?*

A: *Walk him and pitch to the bear.*

9 GET YOURSELF UP

"If you could kick the person in the pants
responsible for most of your trouble,
you wouldn't sit for a month."

—Theodore Roosevelt

W hen you are swamped by overwhelm, it's easy to avoid the things that need a lot of work in favor of the easy stuff. Come on, we all do it. You can ignore the tasks that involve a lot of work because you are busy doing the easy stuff that you can check off your list more quickly. The problem is that often the easy stuff doesn't move you toward your goals or improve the quality of your life. By failing to do the big things that take thought, effort, and commitment, you don't accomplish anything or grow. You can't just do stuff – you need to do the hard stuff.

EXCUSES

Overwhelm is often an excuse or avoidance mechanism. It can be a symptom of some unrest within you that you don't want to deal with. It allows you to avoid taking time to 1) stop and think; 2) examine your environment; and 3) reflect on your life and goals. Busyness can cause an adrenaline rush that provides bursts of energy in the short run; but the crash and burn when the adrenaline wears off can be debilitating. The result can be frustration, depression, self-medication, health issues, and loss of relationships. But you return to busyness again and again because somehow it serves you – or you think it does. Over time it becomes a habit, then an addiction. You become dependent on the physical rush and emotional status. It becomes as necessary to you as breathing. This dependence is as powerful and destructive as any controlled substance, and just as addictive. But there's no socially acceptable 12-step program for busyness addiction. In fact for many it is the new normal.

How do you know if your busyness is an excuse – an avoidance mechanism? The answer to this question requires effort on your part, but it is well worth it. Do you set your priorities for the day with the commitment to follow through, or do you respond to whoever or whatever is screaming the loudest or what you can easily scratch off your to-do list? If it's the latter, your busyness is probably allowing you to avoid doing some hard stuff or giving you an excuse not to do something you'd rather not.

There are several ways to rein in your busyness tendency. When you plan your day:

1. Be sure to schedule at least a few minutes of "me time" when you can pull back from your to-dos and do something to nourish your soul, such as take a walk, meditate, journal, or engage in an activity that renews and restores you.

2. Be clear about what your priorities are for the day, and commit to them.

3. Establish boundaries and stick to them. Don't be afraid to say no to others who try to draw you into their dramas. When you say no, mean it and stick to it. If you don't, people will see the chink in your armor and take advantage of your lack of resolve.

4. Be certain that when you say yes to anything or anyone, you are doing so of your own free will and not from a sense of obligation or guilt. All tasks might not be pleasant, but choose to undertake even the ugly ones if they move you forward. Decide what is important to you and don't let guilt get in your way.

5. Celebrate your success with a small reward or acknowledgment. The easiest strategy is to have a "ta da!" list. Everyone has a to-do list – or several. After a task or project is complete, rather than just checking it off

your to-do list, add it to a ta-da! list of all of your accomplishments. Acknowledging and celebrating accomplishments is the fuel that keeps you going. It is a *physical* manifestation of what you spend hours of *mental* energy doing. It's a simple reward you can give yourself for a job well done.

We often forget to celebrate our victories, but it's a great way to fight procrastination, even if your celebration is to spend fifteen minutes cleaning off a bookshelf. Sometimes one of my arms is longer than the other from patting myself on the back. Patting yourself on the back allows you to *feel* that you've made progress on that mile-long to-do list. If you don't celebrate your victories, you're just on a treadmill and you're constantly going, going, going and you can't stop, and you can't find the control button. Actually say to yourself, "That was a lot of work," and pat yourself on the back, or "I didn't get as much done as was on my list today, but I did these two things and I am darn glad that I did." You don't have to go out and buy yourself a mink coat, but acknowledge when you have these little victories because it keeps your motivation going.

Now for some serious introspection: Would you feel guilty if you had a great life? Are there people in your sphere of influence (family, friends, colleagues) who would resent your success? Would you feel shame or guilt if you were more successful than those around you? Fear of success can be just as destructive as fear of failure. Just let this idea percolate for a while. We'll get back to it.

IDLENESS

Our society eschews idleness. You are expected to be constantly doing something. My grandfather used to say, "Idle hands are the devil's playthings." In my family there was no valid excuse for doing nothing; you had to be always doing something. From an early age I was a "human doing" rather than a human being.

Neuroscience has shown that our brains are most open to inspiration and creativity when we are at our most idle. Great works of invention and art were created during leisure, not during busyness. Have you ever been wrestling with the solution to a problem when a friend called and you engaged in idle chatter about this and that, and when you returned to the problem after your phone call you had a new idea, a new perspective, or a new thought that seemed to come out of nowhere? By letting go of the pressure of finding a solution you allowed your mind the space and freedom to do what it does best: think and create. Solutions often appear as if by magic, but it's not magic; it's your creativity and brilliance emerging from the distraction of busyness. Idleness and wonder are crucial elements of human development and flourishing. You need time to just be – not do anything, just be. Just be it!

ASKING FOR HELP

Part of overcoming overwhelm and shedding the cloak of busyness is developing the courage to ask for and accept help. Neuroscientists call it emotional strength. A component of emotional strength is the ability to depend on others and recognize your needs and limitations; to ask for help. Everyone has a need for independence, which by definition implies the necessity of dependence. The key is knowing which is which and when you should hold them and when you should fold them.

Much has been written about the importance of delegating tasks to ease busyness and become more productive. Try the exercise below using your to-do list. If you have one for work and one for home, do two exercises, one for each list.

1. Identify what you do best and what you enjoy doing.

2. Identify what must be done. It is important to distinguish the "must be dones" from the "would like to dos."

3. Ask for help with the rest. Hire someone, or trade with a friend or a coworker – you do something from their list and they do something

from yours. Hire a kid from the neighborhood to do the weeding or shovel the snow. Split carpool or errand duty with a friend.

4. Openly and warmly receive the help that is given. Don't feel guilty for not doing everything yourself. Each of us has our own unique talents, and the world is a better place because of it. For example, my artistic talent is limited to "I know what I like when I see it"; however, my creativity explodes when trying to solve complex problems.

You don't have to eat the whole elephant yourself! You can find friends, coworkers, employees, or hired help for specific tasks. Get comfortable with asking for and receiving help.

Overwhelm may be a part of modern life, but you don't have to sign up for it. Review the causes of your overwhelm. Are you being realistic about what one human being can do in a twenty-four-hour period? When you are frantically trying to get stuff done, look inside yourself. Is there something going on that you are trying to avoid? Perhaps an issue that is too scary to face? Take some time and be honest with yourself. Identify what you're doing that's stupid, a waste of time, not in alignment with your goals, or not giving you the results you want, and *stop doing it*.

QUITTING

When the going gets tough, successful people keep going. That is not to say that reevaluation and/or adjustment of your plan is unnecessary if what you're doing is not serving you or your goals. Before the hounds of hell come after me, I want to make it clear that I do *not* mean quit if it gets hard or unpleasant. That's precisely when you should not quit. But reevaluating is another story. When you have a project to do, you ideally formulate a plan, then you begin to execute the plan. If somewhere along the way there is a snafu or an unexpected complication, do you quit the project? Absolutely not. The way to proceed is to reevaluate the plan. Thomas Edison once noted that he didn't fail numerous times to invent the light bulb, he just found out how many ideas for it did not work. The key is to rethink the plan, not ditch the goal.

In my life I not only have plans A, B, and C, but also Q, R, and S. At some point you might need to reassess the feasibility of your initial goal, but not before you have tried at least plan D. Busyness is your choice. It takes a lot of energy just *being* busy, and a lot more *doing* busy. Much of that energy can be applied to more productive activities rather than wasted on non-productive and non-gratifying ones. Ask yourself why you are busy. What reward do you get from your busyness? Because, trust me, if you weren't getting something out of it, you wouldn't keep doing it. Are you avoiding facing an issue by being too busy to address it? What must you do, and for what can you enlist the help of others?

Q: *Why did the elephant take toilet paper to the party?*

A: *Because he was a party pooper.*

10 *FEAR*

"Fear keeps us focused on the past or worried about the future. If we can acknowledge our fear, we can realize that right now we are doing okay. Right now, today, we are still alive, and our bodies are working marvelously. Our eyes can still see the beautiful sky. Our ears can still hear the voices of our loved ones."

—Thich Nhat Hanh

INSTINCTUAL FEAR

Fear is a basic human emotion. It has kept humans alive for millennia. When a saber-toothed tiger chased our ancestors, instinctual fear made them run away. Fear stimulates the *fight, flight, or freeze response*. It releases chemicals in the brain that provide the extra energy needed to face the threat. Once the threat has disappeared, the body returns to its pre-fear state, respiration and heart rate slow, and chemical levels return to normal.

All too often today people are in a constant state of fear. Instead of reacting to actual danger, they react to every form of emotional stress as if it were a physical attack. This constant state of stimulation is hazardous to our health and general well-being. The human body was not meant to be constantly on edge.

Fear is usually rooted in the unknown. When faced with an unfamiliar situation, most people's default emotion is fear. Once fear sets in, the tendency is to imagine the worst-case scenario. That is all the ego needs to take a wild ride into the land of "what if?" It's a trip down Space Mountain with a boogeyman lurking around every turn, ready to pounce as soon as you let down your guard. And all of this is accompanied by the music to *It's a Small World* relentlessly playing in the background. No wonder you feel overwhelmed from that kind of pressure. In order to solidify its position of control, the ego is on constant alert for danger, most of it imagined. Soon the feeling of fear snowballs, becoming more consuming the longer it is allowed to continue. The cycle is usually broken by another crisis taking its place, and on and on it goes without relief or respite. Your ego has you by the throat and is in total control of your life. One of the jobs of the ego is to keep you safe. To the ego, *safe* means maintaining the status quo even if it is painful. The known pain is preferable to the unknown. Fear of the unknown drives the ego to be tenacious in its efforts to protect you. The ego is in a constant state of alert for any sign of real or perceived uncertainty, change, or discomfort. If left unchecked it will prevent you from taking the risks necessary for growth.

You can see how destructive this constant state of arousal is both physically and emotionally, but what can you do to short-circuit your ego? First decide if you want to be an actor or a reactor in your life.

LEARNED FEAR

Fear can force you into one of two traps – the ones you make for yourself, often rooted in the past; and the ones that others lay for you, often in their expectations. A common trap is thinking that because something happened (or didn't happen) in the past, it is destined to happen that way forever. As a child, it is impossible to fully understand why something happened, so kids tend to assume why it happened. A very common example of this is divorce. When parents divorce, children are often not told definitively why, and they assume it is because of them. They conclude that if they had they been "better" – however they define that, their mom and dad would still be together. Without another frame of reference, that becomes fact. That fact follows them around for life and becomes self-perpetuating. They have constant inner chatter nagging them as adults that they need to be better or that they aren't good enough. The strength of the story increases as time passes and takes on a life of its own until it becomes a self-imposed barrier to growth and happiness. They are afraid to have relationships, change jobs, try new things, or indulge their curiosity, all because as children they thought their parents divorced because they weren't good enough kids.

This is the very sad kind of trap you can become mired in without even realizing it. It was not a conscious decision you made, it was how you saw your world. But you don't have to keep living your same story. More about that below.

The second kind of trap that learned fear can cause is one that someone else lays for you. It can begin when you are a child and your family makes its expectations known. They can be as innocuous as "work hard," "do well in school," "be safe," "be kind," and "don't talk to strangers." These "whats" are fairly benign. The big traps come with the "hows." Everyone has their own idea about *how* you should meet their expectations. For example, "work hard" is a basic tenet of society. There is nothing wrong and most things right with "hard work." It is when others dictate how you should work hard that the stories begin to grow. "If you don't work hard and don't do well in school, you'll be a bum on the streets." "Unless you spend at least three hours every day practicing soccer, you'll never make the team." "If you don't get all A's and get into a good college, you won't amount to anything in life."

Others' expectations are most often that you should be *doing* something. Consequently you become a "human doing," trying to please people whose agendas might or might not coincide with yours. Unfortunately by the time you discover this – and some people never do – the old stories have become part of your psyche.

You don't have to live your life the way others want you to. In fact, you don't have to do anything the way others want you to. You don't have to be afraid to try new things. Sit with that for a while. Is it true? Do you really believe it? If so, test it out. Do some wild and revolutionary thing. Take a shower at night instead of in the morning as you always do. Drive to work by a different route. Drink red wine with fish, or wear white shoes after Labor Day. How does that make you feel? If it didn't send you screaming into the street, think of your own rebellious acts to try.

In addition to the traps we set for ourselves and those set for us by others, there are ones set by society. The media knows that to keep the public interested and sell goods, services, and newspapers, the stories must be dramatic. The more horrendous, the better. "If it bleeds, it leads." "If they cry, they'll buy." We are conditioned to see everything as a crisis. For example, a local television station declares "yellow alert" days when the forecast is for rain – not monsoon rain, mind you, but showers rain. "Red alert" days are for more than two inches of snow. There is nothing, however, for tornado warnings. To catastrophize the ordinary is to minimize the extraordinary. How often do you catastrophize the ordinary? It is no wonder that people refuse to evacuate their homes when severe weather is forecast; there are so many false alarms that it is impossible to know which threats are real dangers and which are inconveniences. The downside of this relentless focus on crisis is the tendency to see life as one crisis after another, when in fact it's just life.

Life is good times and bad times; that's just the way it is. If there weren't bad times it would be impossible to appreciate the good ones. And yes, Chicken Little, the sky has fallen a million times before, but with each new apocalypse all of the previous apocalypses have worked themselves out. They are gone, and all that worrying and fear were for nothing.

FEAR OF CHANGE

Another big cause of fear is change. Regardless of whether positive or negative, or what aspect of your life is changing, change can certainly be painful. Human beings don't like change. Some people are so resistant to change that they choose to remain miserable rather than making a change to improve their situation. I know some people like that, and I'll bet you do, too.

I had a client who was a victim of domestic violence. As is all too common, she refused to press charges against her husband after each emergency room visit. And he was always sorry after he beat her. Regardless of counseling, legal advice, and a protective order, she was convinced that her life without her husband would be much worse than life with him. She was more afraid of the changes involved in leaving the abusive situation than she was of remaining a human punching bag. After countless broken bones and four concussions, the police found a witness who testified against the abusive husband, resulting in his prison sentence. She is waiting for him to return home when he is released.

I am reminded of the Robert Frost poem called "The Road Not Taken." How tragic it must be to come to the end of your life and feel regret about what you coulda, shoulda, woulda done. Even though change is frightening and painful, you have to decide for yourself whether the pain and fear of changing your patterns are worth having a more fulfilling life. Conversely, is the pain of change worse than the suffering of staying the same?

What do you fear the most? Why are you unhappy with your current situation? Do not dismiss these questions too easily; they can provide valuable insight. You might find that the reason you're resisting change has to do with the uncertainty of having the freedom to succeed or fail on your own. Freedom means taking personal responsibility for who you are and what you do, and that can be very scary. It can mean breaking away from the crowd. It can mean alienating friends and family. But it can also mean having the joy that you've never imagined you would have. Only you can decide if living in fear is worth it.

PLAYING TOO SMALL

If you don't feel at least a little bit of fear about reaching your goals, you are playing too small and staying in the safe zone. What is holding you back? Are you afraid of being criticized? You will be. Everybody who tries something new is open to criticism. Consider the source, however. Are those who criticize you doing so because they are jealous of your courage to try something different? Do they have your best interests at heart? Do they not want you to get ahead? Criticism will come, but it will not be worse than the negative self-talk you are mired in when you stay stuck.

Just as the best defense is a good offense, you can encourage your ego to relax a bit by reducing its self-sabotage:

1. Have a positive attitude toward new challenges; see them as opportunities for growth, not sources of anxiety.

2. Consider all possible outcomes before you start your plan. By minimizing the chance of a

surprise, your anxiety level will diminish and your ego will perceive less fear.

3. Determine what is the worst thing that could happen. What you imagine is probably worse than what will actually happen. By facing the worst-case scenario in advance, you minimize its power.

4. Have a plan B (and C and D) in the wings in case an adjustment needs to be made. This also reduces your ego's perception of fear.

Test this out on your ego. Do one thing this week that is out of your comfort zone. How did it go? How did you feel?

Another reason you might be reluctant to take bold action on your dreams is the fear that you're not ready yet. You need to do more research, have a bigger nest egg, wait for the moon to be in the seventh house and Jupiter to align with Mars. The truth is you will never be ready. There will always be something more you can do to prepare. But you *can* decide that you are *ready enough*. For months this book was in me – actually, make that years – but I had to do more research, then I needed a better outline, then I needed huge blocks of time, then I didn't know which order the chapters should be in, and on and on. Had I cut the crap and just started to write without waiting to be ready, I'd be on my second book by now.

You will never be as ready as you think you should be, which means you will never start; you will never do anything. If you're content with that, fine. Most people are not content with that for long because it eats away at your self-esteem, your sense of self-worth, and ultimately your soul. If you see yourself as a failure because you're unable to accomplish what you want to, that takes away from your spirit and diminishes your soul, just as criticism from other people does. In fact, self-criticism and negative self-talk are much more damaging than outside criticism. If somebody says to you, "Boy, are you a jerk," you just hear it once and can brush it off. But if you're constantly saying to yourself, "You're a jerk, you're a jerk, you're a jerk," that works internally in your head, and you can't combat it because often you don't even recognize you're having that internal conversation.

To get a handle on your fear, ask yourself:

- What am I afraid of?
- What makes me panic?
- What actions do I repeat over and over, getting the same unsatisfying result?
- What am I fooling myself about?
- If I were to try something new, what would it be?

How can you overcome fear? Unless you stop putting yourself out in the world altogether or completely stop trying things that might not work, the answer is you can't. Fear is hardwired in your DNA. You can, however, get comfortable with the feeling of fear – not the saber-toothed-tiger-chasing-you kind of fear, but fear of the unknown. The military has a saying that if something doesn't involve loss of life, loss of limb, or loss of eyesight, it is not a crisis. While I would include a couple of additional items, that about sums it up. Saying the wrong thing, getting lost on the way to an important meeting, and spilling soup on your shirt are not crises. No one has ever died of embarrassment (although from time to time I've given it my best shot). Be willing to give up certainty, especially since so few things are certain (death and taxes come to mind). Move away from the safety of the harbor and sail out to where you don't know all the answers. If you're afraid, and you should be a little afraid, put on your orange Coast-Guard-approved lifejacket and enjoy the ride; you won't regret it. Most important, remember that your *problems* and how you respond to them are the issue; *you* are not the issue. Rather than trying to get rid of fear, learn to dance with it. Let it lead you by the hand to a great new world. Listen to the music of your soul and know that fear will destroy you only if you let it. Fear is not the enemy. How you react to fear is always your choice.

Choose wisely.

Q: *What is an elephant that doesn't matter?*

A: *An irrelephant.*

11 *RESISTANCE*

"Avoiding danger is no safer in the long run than outright exposure. The fearful are caught as often as the bold."

—Helen Keller

The most common reaction to fear is resistance. Resistance is often referred to as "the enemy within." Its sole job as the agent of the ego is to keep you from taking risks. It protects you from things that are too much to handle, have uncertain results, or appear too risky. Resistance is an automatic and unconscious process. Human beings do not like change, and the automatic response is to resist it. Change is so traumatic that people often choose to remain miserable doing what they're doing rather than trying to make their lives better. Resistance is the reason. It is a deeply rooted defense mechanism that is always on the lookout for trouble, whether you realize it or not. Resistance is normal, and everyone has it. It is a basic element of the human defense mechanism, is central to your functioning, and necessary for your survival. If resistance were a conscious activity, it would be much easier to identify and to stop. It is so intrinsic to human nature that most of the time you are unaware that it is in play.

When your resistance is high, however, the best self-help in the world won't make a dent in its armor. The problem is that you resist most what you need to examine most. Resistance is higher the more personal and central the issue is to you. It is self-generated and self-perpetuated. It arises from within like Old Faithful – unpredictable, uncontrollable, and powerful. Resistance has no scruples. It will use any device available to keep you from going forward. It will lie, seduce, bully, threaten, rationalize – whatever is necessary to divert you from your mission.

The good news is that resistance has no strength of its own. All of its energy comes from your ego, which feeds it with the power of your fear. The greater the fear, the stronger the resistance. The more important the goal is to you, the more fear you feel. The stuff that is not important to you evokes little resistance, but the important things elicit strong responses. Like a marathon runner, the closer you get to the finish line, the more your resistance kicks in and launches extra effort to push you away from crossing that line. Don't be surprised by its last-ditch sneak attack; it's only being what it is. Your job is to recognize it and stand your ground.

When others see you fighting and overcoming your resistance, they might try to sabotage your progress because they are struggling against their own resistance and are jealous of your ability to overcome it and move forward. Struggles against resistance can become ugly and even hurtful. Be an example that resistance can be overcome, and don't get sucked in to someone else's sabotage; it will serve neither of you. A few years ago the Powerball lottery hit $300 million. I mentioned to a client that contrary to my custom and belief I planned to buy a ticket. She said, "I already bought my tickets, and if I don't win, I don't want you to win either." The possibility that an acquaintance might win the money caused her to be jealous of something that hadn't even happened yet. I wished her good luck, and walked away. Needless to say, neither of us won.

Resistance can manifest itself in many ways, the most common of which is procrastination because it is the easiest one to rationalize. Scarlett O'Hara's "Tomorrow is another day" was tailor-made for the procrastinator. Without even trying you can find dozens of things you would rather do than eat the elephant. It is far too easy to find diversions, and procrastinating minds can rationalize each and every one. But once you fall into the resistance trap, it can easily become a habit that results in putting off not only your routine tasks, but your goals and your life as well. The procrastinator doesn't acknowledge that every moment is precious – an opportunity to change their life, help others, or create something magnificent. When you learn that every moment is precious, resistance is easier to deal with.

Rationalization is the hit man for resistance. Its purpose is to keep shame at bay. "I don't want to work today; it's sunny and warm outside and the flower beds really need weeding." "I worked hard yesterday; I'm entitled to a day off." "The dust bunnies are so big I have black-and-blue ankles; I have to clean this place before I can work." These rationalizations (read: excuses) are not frivolous, but they are all ways to keep you from eating your elephant.

Rationalizations can make you feel better about not doing your work, but accept them for what they are: diversions. Wait! Before you throw this book across the room... all the activities in the rationalizations above are legitimate parts of daily life; I am neither criticizing nor minimizing their importance. My point is that work time is for work, play time is for play, and domestic-diva time is – well, you get the idea.

How do you know when your rationalizations are merely excuses? Try this: What is one thing that has been on your to-do list for a while that you haven't done? Why? List everything you can think of. Now go back and look at your answers. Which are legitimate reasons and which are excuses? Without seeing your list, I'll bet 98 percent of them (the dog ate your project, you ran out of time, life got in the way, etc.) are excuses. The only *reason* the job is unfinished is that you didn't do it. Accept it. Deal with the excuses by prioritizing or being honest with yourself. This is a powerful exercise – don't skimp on it.

Creating drama in your life is another symptom of resistance. By diverting attention away from your elephant and toward self-engineered drama, resistance once again carries the day. It's easy to create drama. Drama is often just resistance disguised as interesting or attention-getting busyness.

Sit in a quiet place, take several deep breaths, and relax. What feelings do you avoid? What feelings or actions are you resisting? What do you feel anxious about? Is there a pattern in your avoidance?

Neuroscientific research has shown that these anxious states are temporary, and usually last no more than ninety seconds if not fed by negative thoughts or fear. Try to ride them out like a wave – do not give in to them. Do not let your anxiety own you or thwart your happiness. This is difficult at first. You might not make it for ten seconds, but keep at it. It does get easier. Soon it will be an automatic response.

Q: *Why did the elephant cross the road?*

A: *It was the chicken's day off.*

12 PROCRASTINATION: THE DISEASE OF DISHONESTY

"Procrastination is one of the most common and deadliest of diseases, and its toll on success and happiness is heavy."

—Wayne Gretzky

Procrastination manifests itself as making excuses for not doing what needs to be done under the guise of reasons. The task can be so monumental that you don't know where to start, so you don't; or maybe the task is not among your favorites, so you look for anything else to do instead; or you might worry that the project will take too long, is too hard, or won't be worth the effort; or fear gets in the way. Procrastination makes it impossible to eat your elephant, which results in further overwhelm.

Procrastination is not your friend; it is an innocuous name for an insidious villain that robs you of productivity and self-esteem. Everyone procrastinates about some things because we try to jam thirty-plus hours' worth of stuff into a twenty-four-hour day. We think, "I don't need eight hours of sleep; I can get up in the middle of the night and do this," which merely fuels the procrastination fire because when we feel overwhelmed or are exhausted, we can't do the work. We put it off, and all of a sudden not being able to do the work becomes a reason rather than an excuse.

It's innately possible for all of us to procrastinate, but there are some people who fall into the trap more readily than others. Some find procrastination a safe haven for not doing what they want to do or what they think they should do. While no one is a procrastinator at birth, once you get thrown into society and you see how things work and how other people operate it's very easy to pick it up and adopt it as your own.

PROCRASTINATION TAKES A TOLL

Procrastination takes a toll on your psyche. You know how you feel when you don't get your work done, and the effect it has on your self-esteem and pride can be devastating. People often say, "Well, it's no big deal. I can do it another time." But it is a big deal.

A client of mine worked at a large corporation that was perpetually faced with impending layoffs. The company was rightsizing, downsizing – whatever the euphemism du jour was. It never ceased to amaze her that every time it happened, employees were surprised. Even though they knew it was coming, they had waited until the last minute to accept that change was afoot. She wondered why even when people knew that something big was coming, they did nothing about it. When something as important as losing your job or your employment insurance running out was imminent, why did people wait until it happened to say, "Yikes! Now I've got to go find a job"?

There's a strong sense of denial in many of us. We can be born with it or develop it over the years. We don't want to face the hard issues head on, so we might say to ourselves about something as important as an impending job layoff, "Well, that will never happen. They'll never do that. Something will happen and they'll change their minds before that." Some even take the "Well, why bother" approach or think, "I'm going to get laid off anyway, so why worry about it? I'll just have a good time now and I'll buy a new TV while I still have a paycheck coming in."

There's also fear. "Holy crap, I'm forty-five years old, I have three kids, and a spouse who doesn't work, and what am I going to do?" Paralysis sets in.

PROCRASTINATION AT WORK

A client of mine had moved from her home-based office to an outside office, and her home-based office was still in the same condition it had been in before the move. She was frustrated because she is a very organized person and likes things in order. For some reason she was unable to bring herself to clean out her old office. She wanted help to discover what was keeping her from doing what seemed like a simple task.

As we discussed it, I asked whether the reason she put off clearing out the old office was that she was more interested in other things now such as setting up her new office. She also had a big conference coming up, and a big birthday celebration that she was planning. I opined that she had other much more appealing and attractive things to do that got her juices flowing, and that perhaps straightening out the old office was not one of them. The old office was part of how she used to do business, not how she was currently doing business, and it did not have the panache or the appeal that the new office did. This wasn't bright-shiny-object syndrome; she had moved from one place to another and was focused on moving forward and growing her business.

It was clear to me that while this sorting project was not a high priority, the chaos of the old office bothered her. That room was a tiny elephant that she could eat at her convenience whenever she had just a few minutes. If she had fifteen minutes before she had to leave for work, she could sort a bookshelf. In fifteen minutes she could sort through one box. It is amazing what can be accomplished in short bursts of time. And when it's done, it's done – no more thinking about it. This is an example of chunking a project down into smaller, more manageable tasks so as to not be as overwhelmed by the enormity of it. Chunking works for virtually all tasks, and is a key to overcoming the overwhelm of a huge job. When broken down into its components, any task can be managed with much less stress. If you have fifteen or thirty minutes of non-scheduled time, take a bite out of your elephant.

If I write "clean out office" on my to-do-list, the task will sit for weeks. But if I narrow it down to the desktop, because it's driving me crazy and I can't see myself over the piles, the chance of getting it done sooner rather than later greatly improves. When you chunk a job down into manageable, doable pieces, the sense of accomplishment that comes with doing even that little bit gives you the incentive to keep doing the next thing, and the next thing. Before you realize it it's almost done, and then you say, "Screw this, I'm just going to finish it."

You can organize your chunks in several ways. You can divide your task into fifteen-, thirty-, and sixty-minute chunks and do them shortest to longest; sort the chunks by priority; or assign them dates on your calendar. If you're a visual thinker, use the Post-it method. Even though I'm a linear thinker, I'm a visual doer. The wall next to the stairs in my house is a huge to-do-board. Arrange and rearrange Post-its any way you want to visually map out your plan of action. It's like a mind map. You can lay out exactly how to get from Point A to Point B and all of the offshoots, on-ramps, and off-ramps. That's a way to visualize a problem to see where you are and how to get there.

To develop your plan you can you can talk it out with yourself while you're taking a walk or taking a shower. I do my best thinking while driving, walking, or taking a shower. In my shower I have a plastic cup that holds kids' bath crayons. When I get an idea in the shower, I write it on the tile wall so I don't lose a stroke of genius. When walking you can use the memo feature on your smart phone to capture ideas.

Sometimes you need to be alone with yourself. Some people meditate; some people just sit and think quietly because the thought of meditation is a little too woo-woo for them. Let your thoughts move from your head to your heart. That can loosen up a logjam and give you insight into why you are having so much difficulty getting a particular task finished.

You can also find friends to help you eat the elephant. You don't have to eat the whole thing by yourself.

NIGGLES

You probably don't realize that little niggly things eat away at your psychic energy just like big things do. Short, trivial tasks suck your energy away. Just as with the chunking strategy above, keep a list of small tasks (niggles) that can be accomplished in a few minutes, such as "dump the shredder," "change the battery in the thermostat," and "answer that nagging email." It might seem strange to put trivial things on the niggle list, but you don't want the thermostat battery to be one of the seven things in your brain; you have much more important things to think about, and the chance of it getting done before the thermostat quits working are much better if you write it down.

My list of niggles lets me reduce the overwhelm in my head and ensures that when I have a few spare minutes I don't have to wander around looking for something to do.

COSTS OF PROCRASTINATION

Procrastination, especially as it relates to overwhelm, is really about the feelings you attach to your tasks and the level of importance you give them. Identifying the causes of your overwhelm and writing the to-dos down allows you to put the tasks in priority order and choose to act rather than react.

There is a cost in ignoring the niggles just as there is a cost in putting off your big goals. My client's not cleaning out her old office exacted a toll on her every time she walked by the door, which zapped her energy as it worked on her mind. Her internal chatter said, "Oh shoot, I've got to do that, I've got to do that, I've got to do that. But I'm so tired now. I worked a twelve-hour day and I just want to put my feet up and have an iced tea and play with the dogs." But the back of her mind chanted, "I've got to clean up that room. I've got to clean up that room. What's wrong with me? Why can't I clean up that room? It's no big deal, so what's the matter with me?"

If this sounds familiar, not to worry – I've not been in your head. But I have been in my own head. Everybody has the same circus going on inside their head, and we think, "It's only me. What's wrong with me? Why can't I do this?" Everybody has the same maniacal behavior of setting themselves up to feel bad about themselves, and it happens. Chunking down your big and little tasks into small pieces gives you a start at getting the job done, and frees your spirit to celebrate getting each little piece done. Instead of closing the door on your internal chatter – because we all know that if the door is closed the problem doesn't exist – spend a few small chunks of time on it and the problem *really* won't exist. Rather than being tormented by procrastination, you can get many things off your list in short order.

What is procrastination costing you? The most obvious answer is time. The longer it takes to complete a project, the less time you have for other things. It's not just the time you spend working on the project; there is also the time spent thinking about getting it done and about how you haven't done it, and beating yourself up for not finishing it. That time could be used for more productive activities or even for recreation.

Another cost of procrastination is money. This is especially true if you own a business. If you procrastinate about getting a product to market, a speech written, or a website launched, you are losing sales and potential customers. Your expenses remain the same, but there is no money coming in because your work isn't getting out.

For me the greatest cost is my peace of mind. The nagging voice of projects not yet completed sends me screaming into the night. The negative self-talk playing in my head is not only destructive, but exhausting. The costs of procrastination are too great to usurp my goals.

COSTS TO OTHERS

Let's say someone is not doing what you think they should, and you just know their life could be better if they did it differently. What's a good partner, parent, friend, or colleague to do? It is very easy to be objective about someone else's situation, but well-nigh impossible to be objective about your own. One of the tenets of my life is to take people as they are and where they are. You can make suggestions; in my case I ask a million questions (in case you hadn't noticed) to try to help the other person get clarity. I ask questions like, "What if this?" "What if you did this?" "Would it be different if you did this?" "How would somebody else react if you did this?" "How would you feel if you were in the other person's shoes?" Those kinds of questions help people look at the issue from a different perspective. A *parallax* causes an object to appear differently due to a change in the perspective of the viewer; by looking at a situation differently, a solution becomes apparent. Looking at a situation differently than you have in the past – not the way you've always seen it or have habitually seen it – opens new options. It can make someone say, "Ah, now I see what you're saying. If I just did this and that, I might not have a problem anymore, or this would resolve itself, or then I could see a way to resolve it or take further action."

It's difficult to be objective about your own life. This is when a mentor can help you see things not through the pinhole vision that you've had historically, but from a new viewpoint that helps you find your own solution. Telling somebody that this is what they have to do rarely works. Showing them the effect of taking a different action or seeing the problem from a different perspective is the way to genuinely help them. For example, simply telling someone they have to make ten marketing phone calls is not effective. They might make ten phone calls, but their heart and enthusiasm are not going to be in it, and the person at the other end of the phone will pick up on that in a heartbeat. They might make ten calls and gets ten nos, and then feel even worse than they did before. There was hope that one or two people might say yes, but after they got ten nos, they were discouraged, the hope was gone, the enthusiasm was dried up, and they left to work at Starbucks. Showing them how to make cold-calling effective is the better strategy.

In order to get the most out of any activity you take on, there's a threshold question you must answer: "How much am I willing to do and put on the line to accomplish this goal?" If the answer isn't 100 percent, readjust your goal to something you can commit to 100 percent.

If you don't have a mentor or someone objective you can talk to, you won't know what you don't know. For example, if a client who owns a specialty food store says to me, "I'm going to all these networking meetings and it's not working; it just isn't working," I would ask her what networking meetings she attended. She says, "Well, the 4-H Club and the Future Farmers of America." I gasp, "How many of your ideal clients are in those groups?" She says, "I know I should network and go out and talk to people, and I'm talking to people like there is no tomorrow, but it's not working." Clearly this client is not focused on connecting with potential clients. An experienced mentor can help you shorten your learning curve considerably.

Procrastination can be a symptom of something deeper, such as a lack of commitment or a lack of being willing to take personal responsibility. There are commitment issues that feed into procrastination as a symptom. Focus is an important component of fighting procrastination. We already talked about the importance of choosing your priorities, but the concept is important to repeat here. Prioritize your to-do list in order to know where to start.

IDENTIFYING PROCRASTINATION

How can you identify when you are procrastinating, and what are some of the steps you can take to move away from that behavior?

First commit to being honest with yourself, because procrastination is a disease of dishonesty. Say to yourself, "Okay, I'm going to be totally honest – really, totally honest." Look at each situation in which procrastination might be an issue. What has been on your to-do list for weeks, months, even longer? Writing things down is very helpful. When you see why you aren't following through on your goals in black and white on paper, the cause of your procrastination becomes clear. For a day or two, write down everything you do – and I mean EVERYTHING – along with the time of day, your mood, and how long it took you. It might be helpful to use the free template in the downloadable exercises at www.KarolynBlume.com. Yes, it's hard to take time from your busyness to do this, but fighting procrastination isn't easy, and this is the best way to evaluate what to do.

Do you see a pattern? Are there certain kinds of tasks you put off? Why? Write down the reasons (not the excuses) you put off those tasks. What did you learn about your work habits?

Put your list away for a day or two, then look at it again. Often something will jog loose in your head and you'll say, "Wow, was I really thinking that?" or "Is that really true?"

I am an admirer of Byron Katie and her books on "The Work," which is a four-question process she developed. This analysis works powerfully on procrastination and resistance. When you hear a statement or have a thought, ask yourself the following questions:

Step 1: Is it true? (If no, move to Step 3.)

Step 2: Can you absolutely know that it's true?

Step 3: How do you react, or what happens, when you believe that thought?

Step 4: Who would you be without the thought?

This is a very useful exercise to do with any dilemma you face or internal conflict you want to explore. It encourages you to confront thoughts you take for granted or as givens, but which might not be true. We live under a lot of self-delusions, some intentional and some totally unintentional, and we get wrapped up in them. Getting clarity about the validity of your thoughts allows you to overcome procrastination and overwhelm.

Q: *Why don't elephants like to play cards in the jungle?*

A: *Because of all the cheetahs.*

13 ACCOUNTABILITY AND ACTION

"In any moment of decision, the best thing you can do is the right thing, the next best thing is the wrong thing, and the worst thing you can do is nothing."

—Theodore Roosevelt

ACCOUNTABILITY

Let's say you've made a commitment to get something done. What is the best way to hold yourself accountable? If you are a procrastinator, find an accountability partner or buddy who can help you stay on track. My accountability buddy and I speak weekly for ten or fifteen minutes. The calls focus on what we committed to do last week, what we did, what problems arose, and what we plan to do this week. I trust her to say, "Okay, this is the second time we've talked about this, and you still haven't done it. What's going on?" which makes me look inward and figure out if I'm procrastinating, don't know how to do it, or being lazy. Identifying why I'm not getting my work done helps me figure out how to move forward. She challenges me on whether I'm attaining my goals or just stalling. If you've made a commitment to someone else, that person will hold you accountable and they become your accountability partner.

The most obvious accountability mechanism is deadlines, whether they are set by you or imposed by others. By having a drop-dead date by which your task must be completed you can adjust your schedule to ensure that the job gets done. Deadlines set by others tend to have a higher on-time completion rate than those you set yourself. It is much easier to let your own deadline slide than someone else's.

When I set the final – and I mean final – deadline to finish this manuscript, I told several trusted friends when it was. By letting my accountability buddy and a few close friends know that the first draft would be completed by a date certain, I was accountable to them as well as to myself, which made holding my feet to the fire much easier. It's sort of like weighing in every week at Weight Watchers. Publicizing deadlines discourages slippage.

I always ask my clients what they want to be held accountable for. Not what I want for them, but what is it they want. Sometimes they can't articulate what they want or can't see how to get there, so I ask questions. It's their life, not my life, and I am always careful not to impose my views and my way of doing things on other people, but to guide them in finding their own way in the context of their values and goals. Whatever they decide, it is my job to hold them accountable.

Procrastination when starting a business or other new venture can be difficult to recognize. First you go out and get business cards printed. Then you get a website, but you have to put something on the website aimed at your ideal client, except that you don't know who your ideal client is yet, so writing the website copy is very difficult. It also makes explaining what you do a challenge. But you have those business cards, so you have a business. Then you go to a few networking events and people ask you what you do, and then you realize, "Yikes, I need an elevator speech." So you write an elevator speech. So you've done all of these things so you can check them off your to-do list, but you don't have a business yet. You have things, but you don't have a business, because you didn't take the time to understand what it is to have a business as opposed to having a hobby.

Even if you are a solopreneur, you are still accountable as a business owner. If you have employees, you are accountable to them; and if you have customers, you are accountable to them. If you don't accept responsibility for your business, you are doomed as a business owner. Accountability is the best way to keep yourself on track.

Going from the corporate world, where you have your paycheck automatically deposited every two weeks, to entrepreneurship, where you might go several weeks or even months without making any money, is a difficult adjustment. Do you want to sell a product in a retail sales business, or do you want to be in the service industry, or have a manufacturing business – whom do you want to serve? Do you have any experience or expertise in that area? Maybe you have a romantic notion of opening a bookstore with a little reading area and you will serve coffee and sell some pastries. I always thought when I retired I'd open a bookstore, mostly because it would be a good way to support my reading habit. It had nothing to do with owning a business. It was about buying books at wholesale. And that's how some people look at opening a business. But that business isn't going to last if they have no retail experience; retail is a tough nut to crack. When a place like Borders goes out of business, you know that bookstores are having a tough time. This is when a good mentor can save you from a world of hurt.

A mentor, an accountability buddy, or someone who provides you with a different perspective can give you the necessary focus and encouragement to reach your goals with a minimum of angst. By looking at the problem through a new lens, you will be rewarded with greater clarity and less procrastination.

ACTION

More than 1,000 years ago, Lao Tzu said, "The journey of a thousand miles begins with a single step." Your outlook changes pretty quickly when you take action. You will be amazed at how taking the tiniest bite of your elephaxnt can spur you on to take another bite. No matter how small your action, as soon as you see that you can improve your situation or make progress, your feelings of helplessness and overwhelm cannot survive. Fear shrivels in the face of action. Enthusiasm is the medicine of your soul.

Human beings are driven by two things: avoiding pain and experiencing pleasure. Most often it is avoiding unpleasant feelings such as disappointment, embarrassment, sadness, and fear that prevents you from taking action. Perhaps you think there might be some risk, so you allow resistance to step in and stop your progress. The most effective thing you can do when you feel overwhelmed is to take just one small action, even if it is the very last thing you want to do. By making a decision, then taking action, you are assuming personal responsibility for your situation. This helps you take control of your life, which overcomes overwhelm.

For years self-help gurus have told people to love what they do, find their purpose and passion, and do what feels good. This sounds great. But sometimes work is work and life is life, and you muddle through things the best you can. It's called "work" for a reason, and you're not always going to want to do it or even like doing it. Those feelings pass when you take action, feel the sense of accomplishment that results, and are reenergized and remotivated. The alternative to taking action is doing nothing. What is the cost of doing nothing? Be honest with yourself and write down your answer to that question. You have been stuck long enough. You have waited long enough. Now is your moment. Now is the time to beat resistance by taking action.

ANALYSIS PARALYSIS

CONVERSATION:

"Beth, I'm so glad we could finally meet for lunch."

"Me too. It's been ages."

"Hi! Welcome to Tequila Mockingbird. What can I get you to drink?"

"I'd like an iced tea."

"I'll have a diet coke with lime."

"Would you like a few minutes to look at the menu?"

"Yes, please."

INTERNAL DIALOGUE:

"Mmmm, what shall I have? I feel like grilled cheese, but that has so much fat. Chicken Cobb salad is always good, but I'm having chicken for dinner tonight. Soup is good, but they only have vegetarian chili and cream of broccoli. A turkey club sandwich, that's what I'll have. But that has so much bread, and I don't want to spend all my daily carbs on one meal."

CONVERSATION:

"Have y'all decided?"

"Do you have any specials?"

"Yes, we have a grilled lemon branzino with mushroom risotto, a braised brisket sandwich served with or without homemade barbecue sauce, or carne asada quesadillas with spicy slaw."

"Okay, I think I need another minute."

INTERNAL DIALOGUE:

"Well shoot, more choices. The branzino sounds good, but that's a lot of food for lunch. I love brisket, but only if it is really lean. The carne asada isn't doing it for me. Okay, back to the menu. Maybe I'll have two appetizers, or an appetizer and a salad. That might be good. Now which appetizer, I wonder. Oh wait, they have tuna melts – I love tuna melts. But I don't like tuna with relish in it, and I don't know how they make it here. Maybe I'll have breakfast – French toast or a bagel; nope, too many carbs. Maybe an omelet, but I don't really feel like eggs. Okay, appetizers – fried mozzarella, calamari (I'll bet it's frozen), bruschetta – but it's not prime tomato season. Crab cakes are good; so are burgers. Oy, here comes the waitress again. I have to decide!"

CONVERSATION:

"What'll you have?"

All that mental energy spent deciding what to have for lunch. That is analysis paralysis: over-analyzing and over-thinking to the point that you are unable to move on. Over-intellectualization of an issue is one way to avoid taking action, and you might not realize you're doing it. By excessively studying and planning, you are avoiding your goals rather than achieving them. Often you "think" you are doing something but make no progress because you have not taken any action. Perfectionism can contribute to analysis paralysis. Wanting to avoid failure, perfectionists try to think of every possible thing that has even the remotest chance to go awry. (More about this in the next chapter.)

How can you halt analysis paralysis in its tracks? As with most things, recognizing that you are thinking something to death is half the battle. The acronym KISS is appropriate here – Keep It Simple Stupid. Often the simple and straight-forward solutions are the best; there is no advantage in making a problem more difficult than it is.

If you are still thinking, get out of your head a bit and listen to your heart. What does your gut tell you to do? What is your heart saying? Sit for a while and experience the non-intellectual side of yourself. What is your soul saying?

Ask yourself which of your options is in accordance with your values, and which will move you closer to your goal. Then focus on getting started and establish a deadline to finish the project. When you act on a specific issue, a change in your thoughts follows. Being overwhelmed comes from torment and chaos in your thinking, not a breakdown of your life.

$Q:$ *What's the difference between an African elephant and an Indian elephant?*

$A:$ *About 3,000 miles.*

14
PERFECTIONISM: DON'T SHOULD ON YOURSELF

"Use what talent you possess: the woods would be very silent if no birds sang except those that sang best."

—Quoted in *The Ladies Repository*, 1874

W hen I wrote this book, I chunked the chapters down into manageable pieces (duh!), and wrote each chapter separately. After I had written the very rough first draft, I thought what I had was a good start, except this chapter about perfectionism, which I thought was crap. It wasn't really crappy, and got much better in subsequent drafts, but my perfectionism was awakened while writing the chapter about it. Clearly the subject is a trigger for my deeply rooted perfectionist tendencies. I had decided I was going to write *a* book, not *the* book. This is an important distinction; setting realistic performance standards is crucial in overcoming perfectionism, and I learned that lesson the long, hard way. As you read this chapter, notice how you respond to its content

– do you feel anxious? Relieved? Angry? Indifferent? Something else? If a thought or feeling arises, make a note so you can revisit it later.

Perfectionism is a term that gets bandied about like *overwhelm* as though it were a fashion statement rather than an affliction. It can become an excuse for not getting the work done. "Well, I could have finished it, but I'm a perfectionist." Perfectionists hesitate to undertake any activity they fear they won't be able to do perfectly. While procrastination often follows perfectionism, the true perfectionist would never acknowledge that. Perfectionists compulsively and excessively move toward unobtainable goals, measure their self-worth by their productivity and accomplishments, are overly self-critical, and are driven by the opinions and approval of others. They tend to be harsh critics of themselves when they feel they have not lived up to their own unreasonable standards, which leads to disappointment and low self-esteem. Perfectionists strive for perfection but fear imperfection even more. To a perfectionist life is one huge, endless report card of accomplishments and failures, and one failure can outweigh one hundred accomplishments. They believe that others will only like them if they are perfect because they can only accept themselves when they are perfect, and perfection is rarely attained.

Perfectionism is different from striving for excellence. Those who strive for excellence recognize that they are human and make mistakes from which they can learn and grow. Perfectionists, however, see mistakes as signs of personal flaws or defects. Not only do they suffer from failure, but they are also anxious about the *possibility* of failure that has not even occurred yet.

Symptoms of perfectionism also include being highly judgmental of yourself and others, not starting or not taking on projects that you think you won't be able to complete perfectly, taking things personally, and extreme defensiveness when criticized. When you are highly critical and judgmental of others, you are really rejecting what you don't accept in yourself. You see the behavior of others as reflections of your own, and judge them as lacking because you feel you are lacking.

POSITIVE ASPECTS OF PERFECTION

While most often seen as a negative trait, perfectionism does have positive aspects. It can lead to great achievement, especially in scientific, research, and creative areas. The dogged pursuit of perfection has led to breakthrough scientific discoveries; great works of art, music, and literature; inventions; space travel; and the Internet. Perfectionists value and strive for excellence to meet important goals. They tend to be organized and hold themselves and others to high standards.

It is when they believe they must *be* perfect with no hesitations, deviations, or excuses that problems arise. They are intolerant of mistakes made by themselves and others, and live by the "all or nothing" philosophy, in which anything that is not perfect must be worthless. By seeing mistakes as failures, they believe they will lose the respect of others if they make a mistake. And they continue to beat themselves up long after a mistake has been corrected or deemed inconsequential.

There are some things that must be perfect, and some people who are suited to doing such things perfectly. If I have a brain tumor, I want the surgeon to be perfect and not settle for anything less while they are in my head. But when they leave the OR, the need for perfection is not the same. At that point they can ease up a bit and become a regular person with all of the foibles of other humans. You don't have to be perfect in everything!

When I get on an airplane, I expect the pilot to strive for perfection when flying. I expect that the cockpit crew will read the instruments perfectly so we will arrive where my ticket says we will arrive. I expect them to execute takeoff and landing perfectly. Sometimes there are extenuating circumstances, but I want them to strive for perfection. But being out of Coke Zero on the drink cart is not the same as flying to the wrong airport.

At a fine restaurant, I expect the chef to strive for perfection. If I don't like the meal, it can be because it is not to my taste even though it is perfect to the chef. Sometimes perfection is relative, not absolute.

My friends and I used to quilt when our children were little. In quilting, the measurements must be precise or the pieces won't line up and your log cabin will become a lean-to. Quilting is one of the things I choose to do perfectly; but if it's not perfect, I don't throw it out in the all-or-nothing mode of a perfectionist. The little booboos are the way someone can tell it is handmade. A beautiful quilt sewn by my own hand is a source of joy and pride for me. Giving a good speech, even with a few pauses and "ums," gives me satisfaction and is in alignment with my value of a teacher in service to others.

SOURCES OF PERFECTIONISM

No one is born a perfectionist. It is a learned behavior that usually begins in childhood. It can be attributable to parents who put unrealistic expectations on their child to succeed or who withhold love or attention when they don't. Either way, the child strives to do better, often not knowing what better is.

A parent's displeasure can take many forms. It can be overt, such as telling the child that their work is not good enough or lacking in some way. The criticism can come without any instruction about how to improve the work, so the child is left bewildered and disappointed. Or it can be covert, such as a sideways look, a frown, or a shrug. Such responses can be even more confusing for a child whose only barometer for adult behavior comes from the parents. Another parental reaction is to ignore the child altogether. The child tries harder to get the parent's attention, often acting out or engaging in aberrant behavior.

Responses learned in childhood become the habits of adulthood. Fear of failure, lack of self-esteem, and considering goals unobtainable can become life-long impediments to becoming who you want to be. The self-critical voice is constantly playing in your head, and not meeting your impossibly high standards makes you loathe yourself. So what's a perfectionist to do? Because perfectionism is a product of youth, let's start there. When your past calls, hang up; it has nothing new to share. Ever since you gained the power of conscious thought, you have run your past up and down and sideways a million times. It's over. Let it go.

Rather than bore you with dozens of examples of hanging up on your past, suffice it to say that since you can neither control nor change the past, the only thing you can do is change how you respond to it. There the choice is yours and yours alone, so choose wisely. Don't let the ghosts of childhood past ruin the joy of adulthood present.

ARE YOU A PERFECTIONIST?

If you can relate to several of the following characteristics, you might be a perfectionist.

- You have unrealistic standards by which you measure yourself or others.

- If your work isn't perfect, you see it as worthless.

- Every mistake is a personal failure.

- You procrastinate or keep redoing your work.

- You are anxious when you don't meet your standards.

- You are very uncomfortable taking risks because your results might not be perfect.

- You don't enjoy the process of living, growing, learning – you just want to get there.

- You are an all-or-nothing thinker – something is either perfect or a failure.

- You find your value in the opinions of others.

- You are not good at accepting feedback or criticism, and tend to take them as personal attacks.

- You have difficulty delegating tasks to others either because they can't do it as well as you can, or you don't want to lose complete control.

WHO IS IN CHARGE OF YOUR LIFE?

Are you a leader or a follower? For more years than I care to admit, I allowed others to set the agenda for my life. Although I was always an independent thinker and did things my own way, my standards for performance were largely based on the expectations of others (or what I thought were the expectations of others). Not that I was a pushover or easily influenced; I was as stubborn and determined as a mule. But I judged my performance on how I measured up on the someone-else-is-watching-me scale. As preposterous as that sounds to me now, that was my story for a long time. Through that thinking I slowly drove myself deeper and deeper into a self-loathing spiral.

Now I make the rules for my life and I am beholden to no one but me. If you choose, you, too, can be the leader in your life. You don't have to dance to the beat of someone else's drum. You can make your own music. You can choreograph your own dance. You can sing the song of your own heart.

First, decide on your priorities. Go back to your core life values. Focus on the experience rather than the results. Go to the Grand Canyon. Experience the grandeur of Mother Nature at her finest. Relish the majesty of the rocks, the colors, the textures. Close your eyes and feel the breeze caressing your face. Listen to the Colorado River below. Watch the mountain sheep perch precariously on the uneven terrain. Live the experience of the Grand Canyon. Let it fill your senses. Be fully present there. Allow time to stand still. See the Grand Canyon as more than just a checkmark on your bucket list or a picture postcard, because it is. If visiting the Grand Canyon seems too daunting, go to a local park, or the zoo, or a duck pond; find real perfection in nature. In one nonthreatening aspect of your life, let go of perfectionism just for a moment. Get out into nature and be fully present in the experience of going there rather than analyzing its perfection or lack thereof. Fold the laundry or shovel the snow in a less precise way.

What happened? Did the Earth reverse its rotation? Are the neighbors disparaging your unconventional snow-removal practice? I doubt it. Usually the only one who notices is you. So give yourself a break. Give your critical perfectionist tendencies a hiatus for a while and see how it feels. As long as you're grounded in your values, you can let go of perfection and still be safe. No one judges you as harshly as you judge yourself. In fact, probably no one is judging you at all. Your performance is not you; they are two separate entities. A mistake in your work is not a failure of your soul. You don't have to have all the answers in advance; you just need a clear vision. Good questions help, too.

Q: *What is the difference between an elephant and a piece of paper?*

A: *You can't make a paper airplane out of an elephant.*

15 GOOD ENOUGH IS GOOD ENOUGH

"Ring the bell that still can ring
Forget your perfect offering.
There is a crack in everything,
That's how the light gets in."

—Leonard Cohen

Perfectionism is characterized by a person striving for flawlessness by setting excessively and impossibly high standards, followed by vastly over-critical self-performance evaluations and dependence on the opinions of others. The unreasonable expectations perfectionists impose on themselves defy objective evaluation, and lead to poor self-esteem and the failure to live up to their impossible standards. This sense of failure results in feelings of inadequacy, disappointment, and self-loathing. Perfectionists are constantly judging themselves and others for not measuring up. They see life as a constant report card on their worthiness. Instead of being driven by the joy of success and accomplishment, their motivation is avoiding failure, which is seen as anything short of their ideal result.

The perfectionist mindset pervades all aspects of life – work, relationships, parenting, fun, and recreation. In the work environment, perfectionists are seen as overly picky and unfair. Those who work for them can burn out because no matter how hard they work or how good the final product is, it never measures up to the perfectionist boss's standards.

What does a perfectionist do for fun? Although that might sound like the opening line to a joke, there is no humor there. The answer is that they can do whatever they want to, but there is never any fun because the experience is never good enough. Hitting a few tennis balls with a friend becomes painful as images of John McEnroe or Martina Navratilova take over a casual game. There is no fun unless the performance is flawless. Going to a baseball game is no fun because no matter what, their team is going to strike out or make an error.

PERFECTIONISM AND PARTNERS

In relationships, the perfectionist often imposes ridiculous standards on both self and partner. They are obsessed with not failing at the relationship, and seek to have the ideal partner. The partner cannot meet standards that are unreasonable and often not communicated clearly. Because of low self-esteem, perfectionists do not allow themselves to be vulnerable or exposed in their relationships. They keep their emotions, fears, insecurities, disappointments, and inadequacies to themselves, and don't share them with their partner. The partner feels shut out even after numerous attempts at intimacy. Even sex is unsatisfactory since the perfectionist is more concerned with doing it perfectly (whatever that means) than establishing a connection with the partner. When the partner has had enough of a one-way life, the relationship ends. The perfectionist blames the partner for not being good enough. More incredibly, the perfectionist engages in self-blame for not seeing that fact earlier, or for not choosing a better partner. Chalk up another failure.

As a parent, the perfectionist often perpetuates the same treatment that resulted in his or her own perfectionism. Constantly criticizing children without cheering their accomplishments is the perfect Petri dish for creating little perfectionists. Criticism with no instruction as to how to do a better job, or worse, ignoring a child's accomplishments altogether, is destructive to yet another generation. The child will learn the lesson that no matter what he or she does, it will never be enough for that parent. Often the other parent, rather than engage in conflict with the perfectionist, will remain silent and become a co-enabler. Because children desperately seek the approval of parents, and never receive it, they start life out with a very low sense of self-esteem and worth.

WHO DECIDES WHAT'S PERFECT?

Sounds pretty depressing, doesn't it? It is. I have many clients who are recovering perfectionists. Perfection was the barometer by which all things internal and external were measured. The crucial question that I ask every time is, "Who decides what perfect is?" The answer to that one question can turn your life around. Chances are you have always accepted someone else's definition of perfection (parents, teachers, friends, bosses) – as ephemeral as it might have been at times – as the gold standard. You adopted the standards of others as your own yardstick.

As a grownup, you are now the one who defines perfection for yourself, and you have not only the ability but the duty to live your best life and decide what performance standards are in alignment with your values and goals. When you feel anxious about your performance, write down the reasons for those feelings. Look at them objectively, or have someone you trust read them. Which ones are realistic and within possibility? Which ones are unrealistic and set-ups for failure? I'm not saying that you shouldn't strive or stretch, but be realistic, especially in your day-to-day activities.

If you have spent years not being able to live up to impossible standards, it's time to convince yourself that *you* are the one who decides what your standards are. You do not need to be validated by anyone else to be worthy. You no longer need to be in the cage of perpetual disappointment in yourself. You are free. And with freedom comes responsibility. How do you set new standards for yourself that reflect your values and integrity? Teach yourself that good enough *for you* is good enough – period. For a perfectionist, even thinking that phrase is a sacrilege. For them, good enough is never good enough. In fact, to most perfectionists, excellent isn't even good enough. Throw out those yardsticks you inherited from others. Don't abandon your high standards or your *drive* toward perfection, but be content with your best efforts and best results – *your* best, not someone else's idea of best.

When you strive to do an activity well and achieve it, relish the joy and satisfaction of a job well done. The key is to choose in which endeavors *you* want to strive for excellence. When a perfectionist does something extremely well, they breathe a sigh of relief that they didn't muck it up, and anticipate the next test of their self-worth. There is no acknowledgment that they did well.

An insidious aspect of perfectionism is intolerance. When you are locked into an idea of perfection, you cannot tolerate anyone or anything that doesn't measure up. But now you know that in some circumstances, good enough is good enough. You can strive for excellence on occasion, but it's when you choose to, not based on somebody else's expectation or definition. Sometimes the sheer challenge or joy of doing something better than average is very satisfying. The key is being selective in choosing when to strive for perfection and when to honor your own humanness and allow your best to be good enough. Joy is a necessary part of life, and you deserve to experience it often. Live it up! Be an imperfectionist every once in a while, and see how you feel. It will be uncomfortable at first, but try it; you'll like it. And ironically, so will those around you.

If you are a perfectionist, and there is one tag line you take away from *Eat the Elephant,* let it be the mantra that "good enough is good enough." Remembering that you don't have to be infallible or aim for impossible standards is the difference between being trapped in misery and a life of joy and satisfaction.

Q: *Why don't elephants ride bicycles?*

A: *They don't have thumbs to ring the bell.*

16 TIME'S A-WASTIN': EAT YOUR ELEPHANT NOW

"Man is condemned to be free; because once thrown into the world, he is responsible for everything he does. It is up to you to give [life] a meaning."

—Jean-Paul Sartre

Congratulations! Whew! You made it to the end of the book. If you've done the exercises, you've learned a lot about yourself and your world – how you got here, what you're consciously feeling, and how to get out from under the oppressive weight of overwhelm and self-doubt.

If you skipped to the end to see who done it, you've also learned something: You're stuck and unhappy because you're looking for a quick fix and you don't want to do the work necessary to improve your situation. And that's fine, too. My job is not to judge you; it's to provide you with information. How you use it is your choice.

It's all about taking personal responsibility and making a commitment to yourself and your happiness. What does it mean to be committed? Think of a breakfast plate – eggs and bacon. (Mmmmm, you know bacon is one of the essential food groups, right?) The chicken was interested in breakfast, but the pig was committed. That's the kind of commitment you need to give yourself. Take ownership of your situation – the good and the bad. Decide to release the thoughts and beliefs that have held you hostage to make room for the good stuff. Feel bad about the stupid stuff you did in the past; be remorseful. Then let it go, and move into action – move on. Take responsibility for where you are now. You got yourself to this place, and blaming other people or events is a waste of time and energy. Now is your time to choose how you want to respond to the slings and arrows of the past. It's not what you *say* you want your life to be like, it's the result of what you're *doing* that determines your fate. Set aside your pride and admit your mistakes. Then LET THEM GO!

Personal responsibility requires you to:

- Apologize when necessary.
- Be completely honest with yourself and others.
- Keep your word.
- Take feedback and criticism gracefully.
- Take complements gracefully.

- Be worthy of people's respect – you're not entitled to it just because you're breathing.

- Surround yourself with people who will call you on your shit.

- Call others on their shit in a gentle and constructive way.

- Have integrity in all you do.

Life is not supposed to be smooth sailing all the time. In order not to be overwhelmed by negative situations, try this exercise: Make a list of thirty things you can do when life really sucks. My list varies from a quick fix like going for a walk to a major reprieve like taking a vacation. Post your list in a prominent place so it is always handy. Feel free to add, delete, or change entries at any time. The important part is to have visible proof that there is something you can do about it when you think your life has gone to crap. Sometimes just knowing that the list exists is enough to snap a bad mood.

You have suffered long enough. You have the knowledge and power to create a new reality. You can choose your reality by allowing or disallowing certain thoughts to occupy your mind. You hold all the power; you can let all of the horrible things you've experienced and the stories you've created around them taint your future, or you can learn from them. It is always your choice, and now you know how to identify and change your life.

Personal responsibility is a huge part of overcoming or at least taming procrastination and overwhelm. There is a dearth of personal responsibility in the world these days. Many people think that if they put their wishes out to the universe, by some miracle they will get whatever they want. As my grandfather mused, "If wishes were horses, all beggars would ride." Another way to put it is "Wishing don't make it so." The saying "If you build it they will come" is Hollywood, not real life.

You have strategies to overcome the overwhelm that has been an anchor around your soul by eating the elephant one bite at a time. Do you want to shed that anchor now or keep dragging it behind you? The choice is yours.

Choose wisely!

Q: *How do you get down from an elephant?*

A: *You don't. You get down from a goose.*

ABOUT THE AUTHOR

Karolyn Vreeland Blume was born many years ago in New York City. Although she has lived in several states, she is still a New Yorker at heart. She started her professional life as a lawyer with a successful general practice including litigation, real estate, divorce, business, and estates. As a lawyer, Karolyn encountered many diverse situations involving a wide variety of issues and people. She represented Fortune 500 corporations, mom and pop businesses, and everything in between. She has vast experience navigating the treacherous waters of local, state, and federal governments, as well as representing neglected and abused children. She helped spouses separate with integrity while maintaining a stable environment for their children. In her estate business she offered her clients compassion and understanding as well as excellent legal representation. She is empathetic, compassionate, and gives of her expertise beyond expectation.

After twenty-five years she decided there had to be a better way to resolve disputes than beating each other up in a courtroom. For Karolyn that better way is mediation. She founded Conflict Resolution Services, which is a full-service mediation, facilitation, and arbitration firm. With over 400 hours of training – both receiving and presenting – she has helped hundreds of people and businesses resolve conflicts peacefully and amicably. She handled a wide range of cases in the areas of business matters, divorce, elder issues, family disputes, real estate, medical malpractice, and class actions for individuals and businesses.

Believing that all conflict has its roots internally, she has taken her practice deeper to focus on where our pain begins and how to address it. She believes that how you see yourself in relation to the world around you is what determines where conflict lies, whether it be the Middle East or the neighbor's barking dog. She started a coaching program called Parallax Living – Life through a Different Lens that helps professionals explore alternatives to stressful, unhappy, unfulfilling lives and helps them get unstuck by going from "this is what is" to "this is what could be." She provides a safe environment for evaluating your current life and creating your best life.

Karolyn is a known and respected international speaker, consultant, coach, facilitator, mentor, and teacher whose presentations are filled with valuable information and engaging humor. She is an expert problem-solver and a gifted strategist.

She served as an adjunct faculty member at Penn State University, Muhlenberg College, and Cedar Crest College. She moderated a live call-in program for PBS television, and is active in many non-profit and charitable organizations. She is a founding member of Mediators Beyond Borders International, and is listed in *Who's Who in American Law*, and *Who's Who of American Women*. She is the author of the upcoming book *Ditch the Bitch: Silencing Your Inner Critic*.

Karolyn believes that life is full of more choices than you think.

A FINAL WORD

T hank you for your attention throughout these pages. I would love to connect with you and continue supporting your journey through overwhelm.

Please visit me at KarolynBlume.com and sign up for a free report titled *3 Secrets to Never Being Overwhelmed Again,* and subscribe to my free ezine, *Full Blume.* On the website there is information on how to work with me, programs and resources for future growth, and the resources mentioned in this book at the *Resources* page.

Please post a review on Amazon, attend an event where I'm speaking, join me for a retreat, or invite me to speak at your organization. You can join a tribe of like-minded individuals at our Facebook Group, *Eat the Elephant.*

I wish you joy and peace, and a way out of overwhelm forever. Take care and be well.

Printed in Great Britain
by Amazon.co.uk, Ltd.,
Marston Gate.